IN THE DOJO

IN THE DOJO

THE RITUALS AND ETIQUETTE OF THE JAPANESE MARTIAL ARTS

DAVE LOWRY

WEATHERHILL

Boston & London

2006

WEATHERHILL

An imprint of
Shambhala Publications, Inc.
Horticultural Hall
300 Massachusetts Avenue
Boston, Massachusetts 02115
www.shambhala.com

9 8 7 6 5 4 3 2 1

First Edition
Printed in the United States of America

Designed by Barbara Jellow

♾ This edition is printed on acid-free paper that meets the
American National Standards Institute z39.48 Standard.
Distributed in the United States by Random House, Inc.,
and in Canada by Random House of Canada Ltd

Library of Congress Cataloging-in-Publication Data
Lowry, Dave.
In the dojo: the rituals and etiquette of the Japanese martial
arts/Dave Lowry.—1st ed.
p.   cm.
ISBN-13: 978-0-8348-0572-9 (pbk.: alk. paper)
ISBN-10: 0-8348-0572-3
1. Martial arts—Japan. I. Title.
GV1100.77.A2L64 2006
796.80952—dc22
2006019959

FOR DIANE,
though what she wanted with it
I am still not sure.

To see as far as one may and to feel the great forces that are behind every detail . . . to hammer out as complete and solid a piece of work as one can, to try to make it first rate, and to leave it unadvertised.

—OLIVER WENDELL HOLMES

CONTENTS

IN THE DOJO

INTRODUCTION

The writer writes, if he expects to be read, for an audience. As he puts the words down on the page, he hears them being read. He wonders how they will sound, if the reader will understand his point, if they will follow his line of reasoning or the gist of his topic. He also hears, to some extent, the words of the reviewer, the critic who will write about his book. (He hopes they will write about it at least. To be critically ignored cuts a deeper wound than to be panned.) As I wrote this book I sometimes heard the critic in my head, and sometimes some of the readers there as well, all asking the same question: Does this guy, literarily speaking, ever shut up? Does he ever run out of things to say about the most obscure aspects of a subject—the Japanese martial arts and Ways—that is itself about as marginal in our society as a subject can be and still have a presence on the map? As I wrote, I had the distinct feeling from time to time that I was that fellow sitting next to you on a cross-country flight or on some bar stool. The one going on and on and *on* about something or other until your thoughts turned to homicide and then, in increasing despair, to suicide.

In fact, at least one published critic has said that—do I ever shut up?—more or less, about another of my books. I had described in it an *omamori,* a talisman offered for sale at nearly every Shinto shrine in Japan. Why had I felt the need to give the name for these in the book, the reviewer wondered. He had, he explained in his review, been given one recently by someone returning from Japan. It had been described to him by the giver as "a doodad." And he gave every indication this was a sufficient description for him and that my dilation on omamori was, at best, tedious. The book you are holding right now is not for that reviewer. Or readers like him. That is not to disparage him. Or them. The world is full of such people. In certain realms I am among them. Someone, for instance, will ask if I have seen the latest model of some kind of automobile and I will have to answer, honestly, that I haven't the vaguest idea whether I have seen it or not. There are two kinds of cars for me: those that go, and those that do not. I prefer the former and if I am hard-pressed I can describe the color and make a reasonable guess about the number of doors it has. But that's about it. In other matters, however, I am utterly captured by the details of things. I wish to know not only what they are, but how they work, why they developed as they did, and what is the history, pedigree, and nomenclature surrounding them. A friend wrote me not long ago; he had come across the word *lamentation* as a term of venery. "What group of things was described as a lamentation?" he wrote me, expecting me to know. (To my own credit, I did. It's swans.) More recently, I spent some time on the campus of Kenyon College, deep in the heart of Ohio's Amish country and, while perusing the college's justly fabled bookstore, I came across a field guide to Amish buggies. Identical for all practical purposes to the casual observer, each order and each community has its own, distinctive styles. And so of course for the remainder of my stay at Kenyon, I spent part of each evening reading the field guide and part of each day happily identifying the different kinds of buggies that are regularly driven through the tree-lined streets of that beautiful and pastoral campus.

Having spent at least two-thirds of my life around the *budo,* the Japanese combative arts and Ways, my penchant for learning the minutiae of things has not surprisingly blossomed there. I was fortunate; one of my first teachers was Japanese and there were, coming and going through his house on a regular basis, a number of Japanese either living in the U.S. as expatriates or visiting the States, and most of them were amenable to fielding the endless questions I asked. The answers they provided often led to other questions. The questions I had and the answers I received were the impetus for this book. As I continued my education in the budo, I began to make two observations consistently. The first was that there were any number of titles written to explain the combative disciplines of Japan to the absolute beginner. Introductory texts about the history and technical details of karate-do, aikido, kendo, judo, and so on, are all over the place. Some are authoritative and well done. Others are derivative, often repeating the same information (or misinformation) that has come from earlier books. (It is an instructive lesson in sloppy scholarship, for example, to trace the "fact" that Okinawan karate was devised by the peasants of the Ryukyuan archipelago in order to allow them, unarmed, to take on and kill their despotic Japanese samurai overlords. The tale has been repeated in so many books that it has achieved a life of its own and is, in all probability, being repeated right now in some karate class somewhere in the world. Similarly, that the short sword carried by the samurai found its principal use as a means of self-immolation when the necessity presented itself has become another such "fact.")

The second observation I made was that budo practitioners, even some very advanced, even some who were teachers, often did not know the answers to questions about these arts. The training in Japan by non-Japanese has usually been compromised by a lack of linguistic fluency in spoken Japanese. Even if the foreign *budoka* in Japan had curiosity about something, he may have had a hard time expressing the question or understanding the answer. For native Japanese, many of these same questions would never have occurred. The budo have always been a part of the culture there; many of its institutions have just as long been taken for granted. We're no different. For example, we've seen baseball all our lives, yet how many of us have ever thought to ask or to discover why baseball uniforms are basically white or gray, or when it was decided that three strikes would constitute an out? Likewise, as the budo were established in Japan, there would be questions for which neither the Western-born sensei nor his Japanese counterpart would know the answer.

This book is for the kind of person who asks those questions. It is in no way a comprehensive introduction to the Japanese budo. Instead, it is for the curious who inhabit the dojo of the different budo. It is for those who wonder "Why do we wear this?" and "Why is this called that?" It will by no means make you an authority on the subject of the Japanese martial arts and Ways. And it will not in the slightest improve your technique. Only by perspiring and training under a competent teacher and not by reading can one master these remarkable arts. Still, if you are the sort who wants to know and who has asked those questions, it is my hope this book will be of some value. And if you're interested in identifying any Amish buggies that pass your way, I can help with that as well.

I

THE DOJO

You will enter—you should, anyway—on that side of the room opposite what is considered its "front." The reasons for an entrance designed that way are both aesthetic and martial in origin. In the case of Japan, of course, the two are so often interchangeable. The front of the room, where you face as you come in, is the *kamiza,* the "upper seat." Its opposite, the side from where you've entered, is the "lower seat," or *shimoza.* To the right, facing forward, is the *joseki* side of the room. To the left, the *shimoseki.* Thus concludes an exhaustive tour of the traditional dojo, the indoor training space for martial disciplines. Commit these cardinal positions to memory and you have it. Tour over.

If you are amenable to such cursory explanations, congratulations. Japanese culture in general and the budo specifically will be elementary for you. If, on the other hand, you are the sort who lingers on after the tour has been formally concluded, approaching the guide and asking quietly, "Um, could you explain a little more about this?" why then, you have a long and difficult path before you. You will not find your curiosity easily satisfied. You will not discover simple truths. Instead, the further you go, the more tantalized you will be about what waits around the next bend, what further depths there are to plumb. Japan and things Japanese are not nearly so exotic and foreign as Westerners often like to believe. Western images of Japan have often been shaped by those, Japanese and non-Japanese alike, who enjoy making it all seem more mysterious than it is. However, it is naïve or arrogant to believe there is no difference between entering a traditional Japanese-style dojo and going into, say, a bowling alley for the first time. There are profound differences. In many cases, if you really want to pursue what goes on in that dojo, you must be prepared to commit a big, big chunk of the rest of your life going after it. Japan developed as a country and as a culture in ways often very different from the West with which we are familiar, so your path is going to be a little more challenging than if you had decided to follow with equal intensity and effort some Western art. It is, to be sure, a pain to keep on traveling, to keep exploring. It is not an easy road to follow. But you can take it, if you do, knowing you will see vistas, discover concepts, realize truths that others not so inclined to follow such a path will never know anything about.

Some readers will be aware of the two "faces" of Japanese behavior: *tatemae* and *honne*. These are respectively the conduct the Japanese are wont show to the world—the face they put on for others outside their most personal circles—and the real feelings they may have that are often in contrast. These real feelings are never on display and may be shared only with intimates, if at all. Japanese art and other aspects of its traditional culture have many similar examples of what is on the "outside" and what lies hidden beneath on the inside. These are referred to, among other ways, as *omote* and *ura*. The omote of an art are the observable techniques and manifestations of it. The omote of a *kata*, for instance, might be what an uninformed visitor to training can see and deduct while watching one of these sequences of prearranged combat. One sword is brought into play against another, "blocking" an attack in the middle of a sequence of attack and defense. The ura of that same movement, though, may be entirely different. The supposed block may actually be a strike, its meaning concealed by a deceptive distancing between the two practitioners. Or it may be a way of nullifying an aggressive movement on the part of the opponent, forcing him into an awkward position with his weapon that leaves him vulnerable. The point is that when one begins to consider the ramifications of omote/ura, a rose is rarely just a rose. It may not even be a flower at all. And what one sees on the surface is almost inevitably a fraction of what is concealed below.

That there is a deeper meaning beneath the superficial is, as I have said, a recurrent theme that runs steadily through traditional Japanese culture. Why this should be so, incidentally, why it has been so prevalent in Japan, is stuff for sociologists and their ilk. My own suspicion is that such layers are a natural result of a largely homogenous society, where mutually accepted values, expressions, and concepts can be cultivated over time to develop into multiple dimensions. One's status within a given group, as well as one's connoisseurship or sensitivity, could be judged by the number of layers of meaning one has penetrated. It is also important to note that this tendency can devolve into a kind of precious foppery or affectation. "You don't know that peaches served before the solstice are to be cut in sixteen slices and cut into eight after the solstice? How vulgar." The composition of Japanese culture that arose in that extensively homogenous and closed way is a primary factor, I suspect, in generating such multiple layers of meaning. It was also susceptible to this kind of priggishness. The art of garden design and architecture, for example, includes the notion of *miegakure*. Literally, it means "hidden from sight." But *miegakure* carries the connotation of "deliberately concealed from ordinary sight." The average schlub strolls through a Japanese garden, taking in the manicured trees, boulders, lanterns, and such, entirely unaware of the pathways beneath his feet that lead him along. To the connoisseur, however, these same paths offer a lifetime of study and appreciation. Here the paths are smooth, hurrying one along. There, the stones are rough, irregular, or stepped, causing the visitor to slow down. They are a facet of the space in the garden deliberately planned by its designer, who will have wanted visitors to move along at one stretch and to pause at a certain point. The different paths are there to facilitate that. But you have to take the time or have the presence of mind to really *see* them.

With this in mind, it should not be surprising that the dichotomy of the obvious and the subtle can be found (or missed), not only in the arts practiced in the dojo, but also in the setup of the dojo itself. The omote is easy to see. Take a little time and you will come to be aware of the ura.

Understandably, the cultural model unconsciously adopted by contemporary Western budo practitioners in creating their own dojo is that of the gym. It is a reasonable model, since on the surface the budo represent physical activity. The great majority of places devoted to martial arts training in the West are built or arranged in this fashion: as a type of gym. Walk into one and there will be little, aside perhaps from some kind of shelflike *shomen* or *kamidana,* or a portrait of some luminary of the art, to distinguish it from an aerobics classroom. I remember visiting an aikido dojo in which the toilets and dressing rooms were actually behind the front wall, which is, as we shall see, supposed to be the most important part of the whole training area. (Was it just coincidence that this dojo was the coldest, most unfriendly place at which I've ever practiced?) Oftentimes, to be fair, the dojo-as-gym is created not because of ignorance or insensitivity, but from necessity. The group that trains there may share space with other, non-budo activities. Or it may have been renovated, using what space and architecture were available. But in some cases, the dojo is indistinguishable from a gym or fitness center merely because those who make it do not know any better. They seem unaware, except in the most superficial of senses, that on a deeper level the martial arts and Ways of Japan are most intimately concerned with matters of the spirit and not just physical training. Therefore, while the dojo may resemble a gymnasium, its historical inspiration, literally and aesthetically, is that of a temple or shrine. The word itself is Buddhist in origin. *Dojo* refers to a place where some practices of Buddhism are carried out. A room devoted to Zen meditation, for example, is also called a dojo. *Jo* means "a place." The spot where training is actually conducted or where martial arts demonstrations, or *embu,* are formally held is called an *embu-jo.* A *shiai-jo* is a place where budo competitions are held. If you are training outside or in some place not specifically devoted to budo training, you are technically not in a dojo but in a *keiko-jo,* a "practice place." *Do,* of course, refers to a "Way," a discipline, or art. A dojo, then, is a place for following the Way.

It is pertinent to note that this "place" did not, in the long history of Japan's martial arts, necessarily refer to a building. The fighting disciplines employed by the samurai class, from its earliest emergence as a recognizable caste in the ninth century, were largely conducted outside. The reasons are obvious. Few clan leaders, or *daimyo,* could have afforded to build a special hall devoted solely to martial arts at this time in Japan's development. More importantly, since relatively little actual fighting took place on smooth wooden floors protected from the elements, it was counterproductive to train under such conditions. Practice and teaching more typically went on in open spaces: fields left fallow, courtyards, or perhaps on the wide *engawa,* or verandas, that surrounded more sumptuous homes. By the mid-sixteenth century, castle architecture expanded rapidly along with the fortunes of the daimyo; enormous and often elaborate fortresses like the one built by Toyotomi Hideyoshi (1535–98) at Himeji were erected to house standing armies of samurai. Many of these structures included what we might think of as martial arts dojo, or at least large enclosed spaces or halls that could be used for training and instruction. Even so, the samurai spent a lot of time learning how to fight on natural terrain and in all kinds of weather.

Today, while there may be a limited need for such practice (and while arts like judo that require special mats, make it impractical), all budoka should, from time to time at least, train outdoors. It affords a different and valuable perspective on one's art and abilities, and it involves challenges not normally encountered in one's practice. Training outside in different seasons brings the budoka into contact with rhythms, observations, and impulses that have had a long and intimate influence on the budo. This kind of training is called *yagai-geiko* or *no-geiko* ("training out in the field"). If you engage in it, in the strictest technical sense, you are not practicing in a dojo at all. Rather you have a keiko-jo, mentioned above, or a *keiko-ba,* a "training space." (It is significant, incidentally, that in the world of sumo, the training facilities or areas are not referred to as a dojo. The *sumotori* lives at a *heya* or *beya,* usually translated as a "stable," and trains in a keiko-ba, the word used for the actual practice area. The reason? Probably because sumo's roots are not at all in Buddhism but are sunk rather in native Shinto, so the parlance of Buddhism, including words like *dojo,* were never a part of the sumo tradition.)

To return, however, to the matter of the dojo's structural organization, we must remember that for all its outer simplicity, arranged along the lines of a building meant for spiritual or religious exercises, the traditional dojo is divided geometrically into a complex matrix. Let's review: The kamiza is the dojo's front wall—the wall on which the kamidana, or dojo shrine, sits. (The nomenclature is confusing here. The front of the dojo can be what is referenced when using the word *kamiza;* it can as well refer to the shrine itself. If a distinction needs to be made, the front-wall area of the dojo can also be called the shomen, or roughly translated, "upper side." And while it might be called a kamiza, *kamidana* is a more common word for the shrine itself.) Opposite is the shimoza wall, where the dojo entrance is typically located. To the right is the joseki, the "upper lateral" wall; to the left, the shimoseki, or "lower side" wall.

Traditionally, though not always, there is an elevated space against the kamiza wall, a *shinden*—a space where nominally the founder of the art being studied would sit, as would any members of the Japanese imperial family who might drop by. Royalty and *soke,* or founders of the *ryu,* not being frequent guests, the shinden, if a dojo has it today, is therefore a largely symbolic elevated space. Another term for it is *agari zashiki,* or "raised space." It probably came from the cultural need to separate the leader of a family, clan, or art from other members when all were assembled in a house or hall. At one time in early Japan this part of a room would be set off by placing mats on it while the rest of the area was either wooden- or earthen-floored. As tatami mats became more common and affordable, entire rooms could be covered with them, so another way of making a distinction was necessary. Some historians suggest this reserving of a special space in a room was the impetus behind the evolution of the tokonoma, or alcove, which will be familiar to those who have spent time in a formal Japanese house or tea hut. Perhaps the shinden developed for the same reason. It is by no means universal in dojo architecture. In smaller dojo, space is always at a premium. The shinden as a distinct, elevated part of the room that is used only ceremonially is not an option. In larger dojo it will more often be there, set aside in some cases by a short railing. Recently, the American planners of a dojo in a Japanese-American community center took a look at the design of traditional dojo and decided the shinden must be some kind of "stage." Accordingly, their plans called to make it larger in order to "go one better than traditional floor plans" and a bigger stage to accommodate the performers they imagined would be there. Before the dojo construction began, fortunately, a competent martial arts practitioner on the planning committee pointed out the mistake and explained to the architects what a shinden was.

When class commences with a formal bow, seated or standing, dojo members align themselves in order of seniority from joseki to shimoseki, from the "upper" side of the area to the "lower." They convene in the same way at the close of the session. There is a line, invisible but there nevertheless, of demarcation between these two sides. Usually it is drawn at a right angle from the Shinto shrine shelf, especially if that shelf is at the center of the dojo. (The teacher will usually place himself in front of the kamiza along this line. His place is called the *yokoza*. *Yoko* here is the "beam" or "horizontal traverse angle." The *za* means a place where something or someone is seated; hence kamiza, "upper seat," and shimoza, "lower seat.") During training, senior practitioners will tend to stay to the right of the dojo's centerline, nearer the joseki. Juniors train on the other, shimoseki, side. When they interact, the person in the position of initiating the action will be coming from the joseki. In situations where activities demand a positioning of trainees lengthwise in the dojo, the senior position is the one whose back is to the kamiza, while the junior faces it. Or—just to make things interesting— maybe it will be just the opposite of how I have described things.

The floor plan just outlined here is based upon a dojo where *koryu* is practiced. The koryu (old schools) are those arts that preceded the more popular and widespread budo of today. They continue in Japan and elsewhere in a limited way. Given their age and provenance, it can generally be said the koryu and its dojo are apt to have a correspondingly greater degree of knowledge and implementation of such etiquette and layouts of space. Modern budo will ideally follow the dictates of such a classical layout in dojo for judo, karate-do, aikido, kendo, and all the other combative arts that evolved in postfeudal Japan. (Though not always. The Kodo-kan, for example, the home of judo, has seniors and juniors on the sides of the dojo opposite of the way just described above.) However, it is critical to remember: the koryu developed along similar lines in some ways, but as distinct groups in others. They were not ever a homogenized entity. This includes the rituals of who sits or trains where. Local traditions might prevail in some koryu dojo. In some rural dojo in old Japan, senior members sat to the left of the center. In effect, it was the left side of the dojo, facing forward, that was the joseki. Why? Possibly because in farming communities, the eldest son sat to the left of the head of the household during meals. That is one explanation, incidentally, for the expression *sayonara*. It can be written to mean "The one on the left has been heard from." In other words, the family has gathered for breakfast, the father has spoken and so, too, his second-in-command (his eldest son), and the day's activities can begin. From that perspective, it was the left side of the room that might be considered the place for the seniors. Necessities imposed by the layout of the building itself might also influence the positioning. My point here is that one should not assume a dojo is "wrong" if it is organized differently from the way I have described the ideal.

Traditional etiquette, while it might vary from place to place, also specifies such details as the appropriate foot with which to approach or leave the kamiza and the direction to turn first in moving about the training area. Some of these articulations have Buddhist influences in their origination.

One approaches the altar in a Buddhist temple with a particular foot leading, depending on the direction from which the approach began. Turning away from the altar is also done in a prescribed direction. There is rarely any Buddhist reliquary in a dojo, but the custom of stepping to and away from the kamiza on a specific foot remains in many dojo. Other reasons for the stepping in various directions with a specified leading foot have to do with the fact that most weapons are carried in the left hand or worn on the left side. Moving in an expected direction cuts down on the possibility of accidentally hitting someone.

This awareness of where and how one navigates in a dojo has never been a matter of sitting down with a new student and explaining it all. Early martial arts dojo tended to be populated by groups of fighting men who shared very intimate relationships in terms of family, clan, or loyalty to a leader. Japanese culture has as well always been dependent on learning through the process of absorption. A young man entering the dojo for the first time would begin to observe, to see how seniors conducted themselves, and would imitate it. Perhaps a word here and there, a correction or a brief explanation, would have been given. To be sure, these "explanations" might have included a smack on the side of the head or a kick in the butt, all part of *kawaigari,* the "tender care of the dojo." For the most part, however, in a cohesive unit like a dojo, lessons in conduct have always been more a matter of assimilation, sometimes unconscious. (The arrival of outsiders to traditional dojo, especially the foreigners who began training in classical martial arts after the Second World War, placed enormous strains on these conventions. The effects of this change, of allowing "outsiders" into such a closed society, continue to have serious repercussions today. In no small way is the book you are reading right now an attempt to address some of these repercussions.) The question before us at this time is not *how* this etiquette was taught, but *why*? What purpose do these formalities serve? What is to be gained by an awareness and observance of such arcane ritual? In the past, traditional dojo architecture and the associated *reishiki* (etiquette) had at least three functions: first, the placement of the sensei at the front, seniors on the right, and juniors on the left afforded the teacher maximum protection from an intruder. In Japan, with its long, long history of internecine warfare, a *lot* of etiquette has to do with combative concerns. Whether in a tea hut meant for the exercise of *chado,* the tea ceremony, or in the dojo, there was always an underlying concern for protection. Not necessarily for *self*-protection, mind you, but for the protection of the group, which in the dojo means protection of the teacher. Think of a dojo in this way as a beehive, and the teacher as the queen who must be protected against even the most unlikely of dangers. Second, the arrangement shielded the teacher's instruction, coming as it did from the front of the dojo, from those who might peer through the dojo's entrance at its rear. Third, the arrangement reflected, as we have noted, certain Buddhist worship rituals.

These conventions, then, detail the omote, the observable,

readily deducible, and apparent reasons why the dojo is built as it is and why one carries oneself in predetermined ways while inside it. What of the ura? What is hidden that cannot be so easily seen or explained? The ura of things Japanese, as we have already noted, are not unlike the inner mechanisms of any elaborate and sophisticated culture. They are layered, replete with nuance. It is essential to understand there is almost always more to be revealed the deeper and more expertly one looks. Only the fool or the master "explains" with any sureness the whole meaning of that which is beneath the obvious. The latter, the master, is not apt to do so except to those absolutely known to and trusted by him. The former, the fool, provides authority freely—which is about what it is worth. There is little question I fall closer to the fool's end of the spectrum than the master's. And so when it comes to revealing "secrets" I am cautious. It is easy to believe one is sweeping open with a flourish a velvet curtain to reveal to the reader a wide and stunning panorama, when in reality all one is doing is rubbing a fingertip-sized peek through a smudged window—and one that looks out onto an air shaft at that. In the hope of avoiding such potential embarrassment, my approach to reveal at least a glimpse of the ura of the dojo is to hedge my bet by offering not my own insight into the subject but rather to crib one from someone else. In this case, a slightly tipsy tea ceremony teacher.

It was years ago, at a banquet I attended in Japan—one that had gone on for some time, with several courses served, along with generous amounts of sake and beer. So generous that all the other participants in my immediate company wound up getting sufficiently lubricated that I ended up having to drive them all home. I had no license to drive in Japan, no experience with driving on the left side of roads so narrow they didn't seem wide enough to have sides at all, and I'd still be in jail if I had been stopped. But before my adventure in motoring that evening I was at the dinner, sitting next to a chado sensei, a teacher of the tea ceremony. Since she had been practicing chado before I was born, I had jumped at the invitation to come to her home and watch her teach a few days before. This night, instead of her serving me a bowl of tea I was pouring sake into her cup. More than once. The more I poured, the more she talked. I have been under similar circumstances with other sensei of other arts. I have always harbored the fantasy that, plied with liquor, they will let slip some secrets of their arts. It has never happened—or maybe it has and I just didn't realize it. Instead of secrets, she wanted to talk about the baseball team from my city back in the U.S., a team I have always despised. But I was trying. Unexpectedly, she turned to me and asked, "Have you ever considered the Tao in the *chashitsu?*" (A chashitsu is a four-and-a-half-mat tea hut.) I assumed her question concealed a play on words I wasn't getting. But she took a piece of paper, sketched the dimensions of the chashitsu, and then filled the sketch with some *kanji* and lines. While I studied the diagram, she said, "People don't realize how much chado has to do with Taoism. Budo isn't any different," she added. "Have you ever considered the Tao in the dojo?" Then she turned to someone else, talking about something entirely different. And I was left sitting there, wondering.

In the years since that night I have given the sensei's comments some thought. I'm not entirely certain what she meant. Here, however, are my conjectures:

The diagram the tea sensei gave me concerned the interplay of the Taoist five elements, which have to do with, among other concerns, the formation and dissipation of energy. These elements are linked in various formulations to all sorts of phenomena, including time, cardinal directions, and certain human characteristics. On the drawing of her tea hut's floor plan, the sensei labeled these directions and their corresponding characteristics. I superimposed these over a drawing of a traditional dojo. The results were intriguing.

We enter the dojo opposite the kamiza, at the shimoza. If we think of the kamiza as north, the shimoza becomes south. According to Taoist cosmology, south is associated with the fire element, which is, in turn, associated with the intellect and details of etiquette as it relates to human interaction. It is our intellection—our conscious desire to learn—that brings us to the entrance of the dojo. Yet it is to no small degree that it is at the entrance of the dojo where we must drop off a lot of our intellection. It is a difficult, sometimes impossible, deposit for some of us to make. We stand at the threshold of the dojo full of our ideas and expectations about what the experience there will be. Virtually none of these preconceptions are based on actually having had any of that experience. Instead, we have read about it or heard about it from friends, or we have seen the dojo depicted in movies or fiction. In addition to these ideas, the newcomer arrives at the dojo door full of ideas about himself: about his particular strengths and weaknesses, about his special needs or limitations. In nearly all such cases, at least as they relate to the budo, these ideas are all irrelevant. Beginners who appear at the shimoza full of preconceptions must be prepared to drop them off at the door. They should remind themselves that if they truly knew more about what's going on inside the dojo than those already there, they would not be at the door now. They should accept that those inside were once standing at the shimoza as well, equally as unsure about their abilities to make it inside. Beginners are unlikely to get much past the shimoza side of the dojo unless they set their opinions aside and open themselves to the art's teachings.

Entering at the shimoza, beginners find that their initial experiences are largely cerebral, even if they set their preconceptions aside. Without constant cognitive thought (and even sometimes with it), they stumble and are lost. They are unable to do anything instinctively or viscerally. It is at the shimoza that trainees begin to learn reishiki that allow them to conduct themselves with dignity in the dojo, to practice safety in a hazardous environment, and to develop consideration for others. The all-important factor of reishiki must originate at the dojo's door—and ideally continue beyond it when training is finished.

The joseki side of the dojo is at the right or east, and in the Taoist cycle of elements east corresponds to wood and to the values of virtue and charity. The joseki is the position occupied, as we've noted above, by the seniors when they assemble and during practice. To think of the space as an "Old Boy's Club," however, would be a mistake. On the joseki side of the dojo there must be an intensity and a soberness of practice that might intimidate more junior members. There will, if the dojo is a good one, also be a serious sense of obligation and commitment on the part of seniors to members who are not as advanced. This sense is often missing in the modern, commercial dojo. Whatever obligations are felt, they are most likely to be from juniors who will be frequently reminded of their position. They are hit with dues, testing fees, and so on, and are frequently assigned chores for the upkeep of the dojo. They are treated like outsiders and often made to feel inadequate by senior members who have "arrived," and can lord it over them, or at least carry themselves with a superior air. In the traditional dojo, however, the obligations are balanced. True, juniors need to know that their presence means more advanced practitioners must turn down the level of their training in accommodation. Juniors should also be cognizant of the fact that they, as newcomers, have the responsibility to fit in and do their part. Yet seniors in the dojo also realize that the future of their art depends upon successive generations taking it up and perfecting it and carrying it on. Without juniors, the senior students might continue to refine their art, but to what end? Nobody will be around to inherit it. That is why in the dojo the senior practitioners on the joseki side are seen as having an obligation to nurture the juniors and bring them along.

The importance of this crucial distinction as a hallmark of the classical budo dojo cannot be stressed enough. This is particularly so because it is in such dramatic contrast to what we commonly see in martial arts schools of a more modern—or at least less traditional—persuasion. In modern martial arts training halls, especially in those devoted to arts that have a sportive element, the emphasis is frequently placed on developing champions. The goal is to create a cadre of outstanding protégés who will represent the school well and serve as an inducement to bring in more students. The traditional dojo is not based on this commercial consideration. Its prototype is inspired by the samurai unit organized for battle. Think of it this way: If an army launches a campaign with a few extraordinarily talented men in its ranks, it may be that those men win each of their encounters. Their wins, though, don't mean much if the army as a whole is defeated. In other words, an army or a ryu or a dojo are seen to be only as strong as their weakest link. The attention, then, must always be on developing to the fullest those members whose skills are most lacking. In the dojo, that will be the beginners. It is only through the close attention of the seniors that these links are strengthened. That strengthening is always a primary concern on the joseki side of things. The joseki in such traditional dojo is thus less a position of privilege than of responsibility.

It is significant to note that in the Taoist philosophy of a building as a cosmological scheme, the joseki is not associated with power per se. Instead, it is the place from which knowledge and experience issue. Budo teachers and higher ranked practitioners, in whom egotism and arrogance seem to grow well in too many cases, should ponder the meaning of this position in the dojo.

To the north is the element of water. Taoist thought associates it with sagacity. This is the kamiza side of the dojo, the "divine" or "upper" seat, where the dojo deities are thought to reside, or are at least represented. Regardless of a budo practitioner's religious beliefs, the kamiza and the kamidana (shrine) located there is the spiritual center of the dojo for him. Virtually all objects found here reinforce this attitude: the Shinto shrine itself and its votary accoutrements, the tokonoma alcove with its offertory flowers, and, in many of today's dojo, the portrait of the art's founder or some other figure connected to the art. Although some may disregard the "feeling" emanating from the kamiza, there is little doubt that a correctly built and maintained kamiza contributes significantly to the morale of the training hall. Thinking poetically, we can imagine that the kamiza's water element bathes the area before it in the accumulated traditions of the art. It is typical of Taoist practicality to recognize that a focal point such as the kamiza can elevate the seriousness of what goes on around it and assist in directing the sensibilities of practitioners to more spiritual goals.

The left side of the dojo is the shimoseki, which is associated in Taoist cosmology with the element of metal and the characteristic of rectitude. It is on the shimoseki side of the dojo where newer members concentrate their activities. The prevalent quality the trainees must have once they have entered the dojo and begun their education is a sense of the moral "rightness" of what they are doing. They must believe that their seniors desire only the best for them and that the seniors expect them to wish the same for themselves. It is therefore natural that, in the Taoist scheme, rectitude would be the dominant component in the shimoseki. Is the shimoseki less important than the joseki? Not in the Taoist view, as we have already seen in examining the role of the senior in the dojo. The joseki side of the dojo is always under scrutiny from the shimoseki. Guided by their art's high standards of rectitude, juniors watch and evaluate their seniors. Are the seniors' actions and lifestyles in accordance with the ideals of the art? Do the seniors demand more of the juniors than the seniors themselves can do? Seniors can sometimes believe their foibles are invisible to newer students. The truth is that beginners can be perceptive. They can spot hypocrisy when it occurs, no matter how large the dojo. They may not know what is missing technically from the performance of a senior. But watching training and all the other behavior in the dojo, they can draw accurate conclusions about any differences between what is preached and what is practiced. Inspirational posters, framed epigrams or lists of the values or goals of the art; these are mostly found in dojo that cater to potential customers. In a more serious dojo, such reminders are superfluous. The real heart of the dojo is always exposed more dramatically. It is always on display and never more clearly than from the view provided by the shimoseki side of things. Wise beginners use it as such—as a perspective from which to determine whether it is worthwhile for them to continue in this dojo.

The final area of consideration in the dojo layout is its center—the space where trainees of all levels meet. This is where conflict is initiated, engaged, and resolved. Here rationalization, or excuses, however clever or well reasoned, are insufficient. Here, at the center of the training floor, budoka are called upon to produce, to do their best, making no excuses. While this sounds easy in the abstract, the temptation to protect or boost one's ego is almost overwhelming at times. "Yeah, that pin was painful, but the guy was just muscling it on me—no technique." "Oh, I couldn't finish that last exercise—this cold's got me down." "I don't know where my mind was tonight. I just couldn't concentrate." The explanations for every failure or lack of effort come almost effortlessly. Protecting our sense of self, we are eager to resort to them, either silently to ourselves or aloud to others. Yet, at the heart of the dojo, they have no meaning. All that matters here is what we do or fail to do. No explanation is necessary or sufficient. The center of the dojo, the actual training space, is called the embu-jo. We mentioned this word earlier. The *jo* is the same as in *dojo,* a "place." The *bu* is "martial," just like *budo.* The *em* means "to act." The embu-jo is not a place for talk. Or theorizing. It is where only our actions matter. In other parts of the dojo perhaps we can find moments to observe or contemplate. Where there is training, though, what matters—all that matters—is what we do. It should be of little surprise that the embu-jo, which corresponds to the earth element, is identified with the attributes of honesty. For all the pretension that too often surrounds them (or more accurately, that surrounds and indeed exemplifies their pale imitation), for all the regalia and preposterous claims, the embu-jo of the real dojo stands as a heated, sweaty, sometimes frightening rebuke. I have been in such dojo when less-than-serious visitors arrive, people with absurdly inflated and usually self-appointed ranks or titles, people who spin fantastic tales of their accomplishments. I have noticed that such visitors tend to stick to the edges of the dojo, to stay on the periphery. If you asked them, they might explain that it is out of respect for the place. Maybe that is so. I suspect they also sense something about the embu-jo of the dojo, the place where the action happens. I suspect they might realize, even if only subconsciously, that this is a place they do not belong and in which they will never feel truly comfortable.

And so that concludes a slightly dilated tour of the dojo, one with just a bit more substance, I hope, than a simple map of locations. My explanation of a dojo layout in terms of Taoist cosmology is hardly unchallengeable. As I said, it is foolish to presume to be able to explain all there is to the ura side of anything. Maybe the form of the dojo stems not from Taoism entirely, or even coincidentally. It might be more closely related in many ways to *hogaku,* the largely native Japanese methods of geomancy that are even today a regular part of the curriculum of many classical Japanese martial ryu. Still, if there is a *do* in the dojo, it makes sense there is a flavor of the Tao present as well. The forces of the Tao may energize the training hall in ways that are subtle and hidden from ordinary perceptions. As the tea sensei suggested, I'll think about it.

2

VISITORS

O-KYAKU-SAN

If you read the chapter on the layout of a traditional dojo, you might notice an area that seems to be missing. Where do the visitors sit or stand to watch training? In a commercial dojo, attracting new members is a vital aspect for the teacher and the students. Some dojo go to great and expensive lengths to advertise. "Visitors welcome" is a frequent phrase in their ads and brochures. To be sure, much of this approach has to do with the cost of running a dojo. Additionally, there may be a lot of honest enthusiasm about what goes on in the dojo and a desire to share it. There is a sense of "I love this and I can't understand why everyone else wouldn't love it as well and so the more the merrier" in many budoka. The attitude is understandable. But it is unreasonable. The budo, practiced correctly as they were meant to be, will never have an enormous following. It is not that they require superhuman effort. They are not so esoteric and difficult that they cannot be pursued by normal people. But they require a commitment and a willingness to endure boredom, repetition, and a constant criticism that are not in tune with modern life. There will never be flocks of people coming to the dojo, even though after a movie or book comes out that features a martial art, prospective attendance might temporarily spike. There isn't much need for a visitors' section because, if for no other reason, there just won't be that many of them.

When they do come, visitors to the dojo are in Japanese *kyaku,* a word that usually gets the honorific *o-* added to it as a prefix to make it more polite. (Technically, visitors to a tournament or budo competition are called *kankyaku* or "guests in the hall," since these events are often held in larger places than the dojo.) Casual *o-kyaku-san* might be tolerated, but they are never encouraged. There usually isn't enough room for them; they will be standing at the side of the training area and in the way. More important, however, they distract from what is going on in the dojo. They are not serious, and their lack of this is obvious. The martial arts or Ways are a spectacle, a temporary distraction for them. They typically wander in and ask about classes ("How much do you charge?" is an obvious clue they do not have any designs on actually joining.) Then they stand around and watch and begin to shift and lose patience and begin looking at the door and wondering how soon they can be on their way without seeming overly rude. Window-shoppers are fine in a car showroom or a jewelry store. In the dojo, they don't belong and usually realize it quickly.

The serious visitor approaches in an entirely different way. If a phone number is available for the dojo, he calls it. He asks permission to come and watch. He does not say he wishes to join. Why would he? He doesn't presume to know the art or the people practicing it or the quality of the teacher. If I make an overture to join your group without so much as coming by to meet you or watch what you do, how superficial must I be? It is a custom at many traditional dojo that a prospective member come to watch at least three or four classes before any mention is made of joining. The visitor demonstrates his patience; the dojo's activities are revealed to him so he has some idea of what it is he proposes to get into. It's a good way to get acquainted on both sides. Once he has seen several classes and has demonstrated he has the patience not to be in a hurry, a senior in the dojo might quietly approach him or he might politely ask one of those seniors about the possibility of joining.

There are many tales, many of them from movies or novels, about the rigors of trying to be accepted into a martial arts training hall. In reality, the teacher does not make it easy to join, not because he's "testing" the would-be student, but rather because he doubts the visitor really wants to join. Ironically, the harder the prospective student tries to impress the teacher and the others in the dojo, the less serious he looks in their estimation. He should remember that he is not seeking membership into a monastery, not trying to convince some mysterious cabal of his worthiness to be allowed into the inner enclave. His goal is merely to demonstrate that he is mature and, while he knows he doesn't know the level of commitment that will be asked of him, he is open to learning. It just takes a bit of patience. And looking back on it, once he has joined the dojo and begun his study, he will likely be surprised at how quickly he went from being an o-kyaku-san to becoming a member of this odd place.

3

THE UNIFORM

KEIKOGI

Given the popular image of "traditional" Japanese dress—sumptuous silk kimono and lavish brocade—it may be surprising to learn how often people in old Japan went naked or nearly so. Early accounts by some of the first Westerners in Japan—Portuguese explorers—note that the common Japanese were often "naked as frogs." Centuries later, in 1859, the newspaper correspondent and business pioneer to Japan, Francis Hall (1822–1902), wrote that "The dress of the common people was quite as free as their manners. The coolie class were either naked, with the exception of a loincloth, or wore a loose cotton robe open all the length in front and which revealed quite as much as it covered." Almost twenty years later, the adventuress Isabella Bird (1831–1904), exploring in the backcountry of Japan noted that, "The men may be said to wear nothing."

Of course, if we are to consider the clothing worn in *really* old Japan, we have far fewer objective and reliable sources. Archaeological digs into sites dating back to the Jomon civilization of about six thousand years ago uncovered swatches of textiles, but it is impossible to make much useful conjecture about what sort of couture might have been preferred by the average Mr. and Mrs. Jomon. The first record of early Japanese clothing came from the Chinese third-century text *Wei Chih*, which describes emissaries from Japan who paid a visit to the Chinese court. The "Wajinden," as Japanese were called by the Chinese, were wearing clothes consisting of long, unsewn fabric wrapped around them. This would have been near the end of the Yayoi period in Japan (300 B.C.E.– 300 C.E.) and the description is confirmed by the haniwa, the strange and evocative little clay figures that were molded about this time, depicting, among other objects, their human makers. Haniwa figures are clad in what look like robes, some long, some short, wrapped around the body exactly like a kimono or a martial arts *keikogi* is today. Interestingly, the clothes are quite similar to those worn by hunting civilizations on mainland Asia, and they are an important clue about the still-mysterious origins of the Japanese race.

Prince Shotoku, who assumed the throne of Japan's imperial regent in 593, was influenced in many ways by China. Shotoku adopted and made popular the long robes that would eventually evolve, by the Heian era, into the distinctive Japanese kimono we all recognize now. But what of the common people? We see art of the Romantic period of feudal Japan, pictures of languorous women floating in as many as a dozen layers of silk in their fabulous kimono, and men in stately silk robes as well. These, however, do not seem terribly practical or affordable for wear while planting rice or building a house. The common folk in Japan from about the tenth century until the end of the fourteenth wore clothes of hemp. This plant fiber was tough and durable, although it was not particularly comfortable. It was also labor-intensive to grow, spin into yarn, and weave into cloth. (In fact, poorer classes in Japan at that time could not afford hemp and often wore clothes made of thick mulberry paper.) But during the Sengoku *jidai,* or Warring States period, the centuries-long civil war in Japan that began in the fifteenth century, cotton was introduced to Japan from Korea and China. We often think of farm fields in Japan as green with growing rice. However, especially in the Kansai region around Osaka, the green in those fields was topped with balls of white. Cotton was as much king there as it was in the American South four centuries later.

In myriad ways, cotton revolutionized Japan's economy and its civilization. Cotton was easy to grow and to process into cloth. Clothing, sturdy and even stylish, became affordable for even the poorest Japanese. Some historians suggest that cotton clothing, because it could be fitted so well to show off the form of the human body, was a major impulse in formulating the traditional Japanese sense of beauty. For the purposes of understanding how our training clothes came about, it is also a significant development. The keikogi worn today in dojo all over the world are, indirectly at least, a result of the importation of cotton as a fabric to Japan and to the clothes that came from it.

Sumo, Japan's earliest combative art, was practiced and

performed naked or nearly so. Wrestlers wore at most a wrapped loincloth, the fashion descendants of which are still seen today in the *mawashi* worn in sumo training and tournaments. Was the nudity of sumo a reflection of the paucity of clothing in ancient Japan? Or was it symbolic: a way of entering into a contest of strength and skill reduced to the utter simplicity of one's own muscles and nerves? Who knows? But as other combative arts developed, particularly those devoted to close-quarters grappling, "training clothes" were usually necessary. These clothes had to be sturdy for obvious reasons. They had to be roomy and comfortable in which to move. And they had to be affordable for practitioners. Early wood-block prints show jujutsu practitioners wearing everyday simple jackets cut like kimono in fashion but woven of cotton. We might be tempted to speculate that these were silk kimono. How do we know they were cotton? Aside from the fact that silk would have been too valuable a material to have risked damaging or tearing during hard training, formal silk kimono are actually sewn together with a loose, basting kind of stitch. They are not designed to withstand a lot of pulling or yanking. The stitches are easily removed so the garment can be cleaned and resewn. In the case of the jackets worn for martial arts practice, if these prints are any indication, they were not special or reserved particularly for budo training. They were simply the rough cotton "robe" or jacket worn for any other activity.

It was not until almost the end of the nineteenth century that the keikogi as a specific "costume" emerged in Japan.

Keiko means "practice." *Gi* is the pronunciation for the character of *ki*—or "clothing," the same one in *kimono*—when it serves as a suffix. Primary credit for the keikogi must go to Jigoro Kano (1860–1938), the educator and founder of Kodokan judo. We are speculating, but it's a good bet his inspiration was the heavy jacket worn by the firemen of Japan. These jackets were originally made of hemp, and they in turn were probably inspired by the upper garments worn by the *yakko*. Yakko are variously described as "footmen," "valets," or "servants." If you have seen pictures of daimyo or high-ranking samurai traveling in a formal procession, you will have noted men carrying banners or poles decorated in various ways to denote the status or clan of the man at the head of the parade. These men were yakko. (The word, incidentally, lives on in the tofu dish *hiya-yakko*. Cubes of tofu are served chilled on ice, with assorted condiments. The blocks of tofu look like the big white squares on the jackets of the yakko, hence the name.) Firemen adapted the hip-length jacket of the yakko in their profession. Firefighting in the cities of Japan involved leaping on top of roofs to beat out sparks or small fires blown by the wind—an errant spark in a city built of wood and paper could turn a small house fire into a conflagration capable of destroying dozens of blocks. For protection, firemen wore heavy coats, or *hanten,* which are quite similar to the jackets worn in the dojo. Another variation of the hanten, incidentally, is the *happi,* a light, mid-thigh-length jacket still seen at street festivals and celebrations in Japan.

According to the records maintained by the Kodokan,

Kano devised the *judogi* we wear today "for reasons of dignity and safety." One of the earliest photos taken of Kano has him as a young buck at seventeen, trying very hard to look tough by striking a theatrical pose, attired in a sleeveless blouse of some sort, legs naked. It looks more like a Victorian-era swimsuit than a modern judo uniform. Photos taken less than two decades later, very late in the nineteenth century, depict Kano and other *judoka* in their jackets, or *uwagi*, that look almost exactly like the hanten of the fireman. (The Kodokan has preserved one of Kano's training jackets from this period, ragged and discolored with perspiration, that, aside from the shorter sleeves, looks no different than those worn now.) In its prototypical form, these were short-sleeved, and the bottom of the garment was just to the level of the buttocks. Some of Kano's students recalled that mat burns to the elbows inspired Kano to lengthen the sleeves so they came midway down the forearms. The rough-and-tumble of freestyle practice may have caused him to lengthen the jacket so it extended down to the bottom of the hips, making it less likely to be pulled open in practice sessions. A mat full of students practicing judo in a photo dated 1913 of training at the Kodokan are all wearing today's version of the judogi (though a few seniors appear in formal kimono). Another from the 1920s shows the always dapper Kano attired in a completely modern keikogi. We can surmise, then, that the evolution of the training uniform in judo came about fairly quickly, and that to a considerable extent it was altered to fit as it does today for practical rather than aesthetic reasons.

Karate, introduced to Japan about the same time the judo uniform was assuming its present cut and shape, was originally practiced in everyday clothes or, in the humid heat of the Okinawan islands, in loincloths. The karate pioneers who brought their native combative art from Okinawa to Japan were a colorful and varied lot. Some were brawlers and braggarts; others were scholars and gentry. Most, though, were astute and savvy enough to realize that their karate, considered by the average Japanese to be a savage and lower-class form of fisticuffs in comparison with the elite combative arts of the classical samurai, had to be marketed just right if it was going to be successful on mainland Japan. A Kentucky moonshiner might be able to compete with a centuries-old Scottish distillery—but he'd better find something more suitable in which to bottle his wares than a mason jar. Almost simultaneously to its being introduced to Japan in the 1920s, karate training was conducted there wearing a uniform based on the one used in judo. A photograph from 1930 of Gichin Funakoshi conducting karate training at Keio University in Tokyo shows teacher and students all attired in clothes indistinguishable from judogi. Later, as karate assumed its own distinctive and Japanese identity, its enthusiasts designed uniforms made of lighter grades of cotton to facilitate the kicking and punching movements of the art.

What of other budo forms? The earliest photos of Morihei Ueshiba teaching and training date from the 1920s. He and his students all appear to be wearing judogi with *hakama*. Judogi were being commercially manufactured in Japan by that time, making them available and affordable, and Ueshiba doubtless used them for those reasons, along with the fact that they were suitable for aikido practice. *Kendogi* were also a natural development that combined the cut of the everyday kimono with the sturdiness of the firefighter's traditional jacket. The kendo uwagi differs from those of other budo in that there are no slits along the sides as are found in judo jackets. Rather, the split is directly in the rear of the garment. The *kendoka*'s lateral movements during practice are more restricted than those of the judoka and he rarely takes a wide stance of any kind. So his jacket doesn't need the slits on the side that make such movements more comfortable in the judo dojo. Typically, the kendoka also goes trouserless underneath his hakama, because the straight, uncut edges of the bottom of his jacket keep his bare legs from showing. Archery, or *kyudo,* was originally performed in kimono or in battle dress; by the turn of the twentieth century, its exponents began to adopt for regular practice and instruction a light cotton top that was worn much like the undergarment of a formal kimono.

Keikogi, with the exception of those dyed indigo and used for kendo and some other martial arts, are white. (Some white keikogi tops have a crosshatched stitching of black thread running through them or, if they are indigo blue, the stitching will be white. This is called a *Musashi-sashi* style of keikogi, named after the province where the style of textile weaving originated. Women and children, especially in kendo, most frequently wear Musashi-style keikogi.) Keikogi are white because it is the natural color of the cotton of which they are made and so is both cheap and reflective of a certain spirit of simplicity and naturalness that is consonant with the values of the budo. They are white because they have always been so, and tradition, while it is not sufficient a rationalization for all institutions, is nevertheless a powerful factor when it comes to matters of arts like budo. There is no coherent reason for the introduction of other colors to the keikogi other than to satisfy the dictates of changeable fashion or to address the wearer's need to express his own whims; therefore it is important *not* to introduce them. In 1997, the International Judo Federation, not content to have stripped judo of much of its original intent or value, instituted the wearing of blue keikogi in contests, ostensibly to make scoring and following the matches easier. That such shallow impulses have been taken seriously by the judo community in any way is characteristic of the modern iteration of this art, a fatuous imitation of the real thing.

Some parts of the keikogi bear mention, beginning with the jacket itself that we have been discussing and have already identified as an uwagi. *Uwa* means "upper." The suffix of *-gi* is the same as the *ki* of "kimono"; it is, as we noted earlier, the character for "clothes." (An archaic word for the uwagi is *uwafuku; fuku* here means "clothes" as well and it is still used in other terms in Japanese like *wafuku,* or "Western-style clothes." But it sounds odd and a little affected if we are talking about the keikogi. *Seifuku* is the Japanese word for "uniform." Today it is used mostly to describe the *gakuseifuku,* the various school uniforms worn by students.) In some uwagi, a seam, called the *sensui,* runs straight down the back of the jacket, which can allow it to fit more neatly. Many judoka and *aikidoka* don't care for this, however, since the additional seam can make the jacket more susceptible to tearing along the sewn lines. They prefer the *ushiromigoro,* or rear of the uwagi, to be of a single piece of cloth. The sleeves are *sode;* their openings *sodeguchi.* Some budoka prefer long sleeves, which they roll up, making a handy forearm pad for wiping away perspiration. Some teachers, though, dislike this practice and will insist sleeves be altered to fit correctly if they're too long. The *sode,* along with the collar, are the parts of the uwagi gripped by judoka. This particular grip is probably a reflection of earlier seizing techniques employed by jujutsu systems. Kimono sleeves are quite large; grabbing and then twisting them is a quick and effective way of tying up the upper body. *Sode-garami,* or "sleeve entanglers," were pole arms used by feudal-era police, long pikes with spikes on the end that could be thrust into the sleeve area and twisted, rendering useless a sword held with that arm. The current *kumikata,* or standard judo grip, is a derivation of this strategy.

The collar and lapels of the uwagi are called, in Japanese, the *eri. Eri o tateru,* or "make the collar stand up," is an admonition sometimes heard when teaching a person the rudiments of *kitsuke,* or the art of wearing a kimono. By "standing up" it is meant that the lapels should be neatly folded over one another, left over right (the exception is the kimono in which a person is dressed for a funeral; there the fold is switched, right over left), so there is no gaping space below the throat. In kendo and karate, there are small strings or cloth tabs attached, either at the chest level or on the part of the garment below the waist, that can be knotted to keep the uwagi looking neater and keeping it together. Judo never used these because in the pulling and tugging of a judo practice or match, the strings would quickly be torn. The judoka, in fact, has a more difficult time keeping his jacket looking tidy because of the nature of judo's gripping methods. Jackets in a strenuous match can be pulled completely out of the belt, leaving them flapping open. (Some judoka will actually help this process along, knowing that when their uwagi becomes undone, the referee will call a temporary halt to the match, giving them time to catch their breath while they rearrange the uwagi. An interesting ploy perhaps, but it is inconsistent with the values of judo, and those who look upon the art as an approximation in some way of hand-to-hand combat on the feudal battlefield should reflect on just how quickly trying to call a "time-out" in a real fight would mean their death.)

Judoka, if they are being instructed correctly, are taught to straighten their eri subtly, after a match or in between sets of kata, by pulling on the bottom parts of the uwagi, down below the belt. This part of the keikogi, incidentally, is the *shitagi*. *Shita* means "lower." (*Shitagi* can also be used to refer to garments worn under a kimono.) In keikogi worn for judo and aikido, the shitagi is made from a lighter grade of cotton and has a crosshatched pattern distinctive from the upper part of the jacket. The weight and sewing on the shitagi is meant to make the jacket lighter and to facilitate the flow of perspiration from the heavier weave on top. However one keeps the eri closely folded—and it is a matter of learning to move correctly along with practice more than anything else—the ability to do so is the sign of either a martial artist who never does anything strenuous enough to make the eri come apart or one who has been in the dojo long enough to know what he is doing.

In the West, we have been wearing trousers for so many centuries that it seems, from the perspective of fashion as well as of modesty and functionality, that this part of clothing would be universal. In Japan, however, trousers have been a very recent addition to everyday clothing. Westerners in Japan just after World War II recall seeing Japanese wearing pants for the first time who clearly had no idea how to do so. They were sometimes pulled up to the chest, leaving the legs exposed from the calves down, sometimes worn with a leather belt wrapped around the waist instead of fitted through the belt loops, or backward. The Japanese word for pants, *zubon,* did not even enter the language until after the close of the feudal period. In premodern Japan men either went naked from the waist down except for a loincloth, or they wore some kind of hakama. Again, the introduction of pants to the keikogi came from Jigoro Kano. As we noted earlier, woodblock prints and other illustrations invariably depict martial artists wearing either traditional hakama, or with bare legs in their training sessions. Among the oldest photographs of judo or jujutsu practice, practitioners are clad similarly. Western influences led to the adoption of *gobatake,* a kind of loose undergarment like shorts, that came down to the thighs. If you have visited Tokyo during the summer, likely you have seen men wearing *patchi,* which look like a cross between boxer shorts and swimming trunks, light cotton drawers that come down to midthigh. Men relaxing at home or shopkeepers in mom-and-pop businesses often wear patchi during the summer months. It is another garment that can be traced back to the near-mania for Western fashions that began in Japan during the latter part of the nineteenth century and that peaked after the Second World War. Some early textbooks on jujutsu depict combatants in very short pants that look like, and may have been inspired by, gobatake or patchi.

Kano, in all likelihood, saw longer trousers as a way of protecting his judoka against the same kind of mat burns that encouraged him to lengthen the sleeves of the jacket. Additionally, he could see how they might also help define his judo as a new and modern art, one with a universal appeal. This second reason may have been more influential than one might think. The appeal for "tradition" in modern martial arts is, in our era, in some circles, considerable. It is important to note, however, that in Japan following the end of the feudal era, many traditional arts and classical culture were held in contempt, or were at best thought quaint and hopelessly outmoded. A discipline like judo would have had far more attraction practiced in modern trousers than in traditional hakama. Photographs at the Kodokan dating to the first decade of the twentieth century show Kano and other practitioners in zubon that go below the knee. Karate practitioners soon adopted a similar length for their uniforms' zubon.

As with the uwagi, zubon are white, and for the same reasons. They are not bell-bottomed or festooned with insignia or other decorations. They have a unique drawstring, with a cord passed around the front of the garment's waist through a seam in the waistband, looping over itself in the rear, then coming back to the front. It is cinched by pulling on the ends of both cords. The ends of these cords are knotted to prevent them from slipping back into the seam. Nevertheless, it happens and it is just as frustrating as when a string disappears the same way in a hooded sweatshirt or in a swimming suit. Look around the dojo dressing room and you might see a curved piece of coat-hanger wire with a loop in one end. It's like a big needle for restringing a lost cord in the zubon.

And then there is the *obi*. Has ever a piece of apparel been more closely identified with the activity of the wearer? Has there ever been an article of clothing invested with more mythology, more mystique, than the length of cloth worn around the waist of the martial arts enthusiast? What the lederhosen is for the oompah-band player, what the over-the-shoulder sash is for the beauty contestant, what the hockey mask is for the deranged serial killer, the belt is even more for the martial artist. The "black belt" is inextricably woven around the waist of the karate or judo exponent. The twelve-year-old *karateka* wears his green belt with all the pride of a

Masai warrior in his lion-skin cape. At social gatherings, if one's status in the dojo is known at all outside it, one can expect to be introduced as, "He's a black belt, so watch out."

That a strip of cotton used to keep one's jacket closed should have assumed such symbolic importance is curious. It began innocently enough. The official history of judo's Kodokan notes that in 1883 Kano decided to separate the student body of his new Kodokan into two groups. One would be those whose skills or progress were sufficient for them to be considered "senior." They were the *yudansha,* or "graded group." All others were at the lower *mudansha,* or "without-grade group." The register of the Kodokan lists two yudansha who were that year awarded a *shodan,* or "first level of yudansha," rank: Tsunejiro Tomita and Shiro Saigo, two of Kano's most senior and illustrious students. Tomita would go on to demonstrate judo in the United States and elsewhere. A fictionalized version of the exploits of Shiro Saigo as the hero of a popular novel later turned into an even more popular film by Akira Kurosawa, *Sugata Sanshiro,* about the early contest between Kano's judo and classical jujutsu schools. These two were, arguably, the first "black belts."

Kano's implementation of a system of "grades," known in Japanese as *dan-i,* was a minor revolution in the world of the Japanese combative arts and in Japanese arts in general. For centuries, since the establishment of the first ryu, ranks were almost always awarded through a series of *menkyo,* or "licenses." The headmaster of the school issued menkyo, often in the form of a scroll or paper. In ryu devoted to budo, like those for flower arranging or other arts, there were usually few menkyo in the grading system. A license might be granted to signify the recipient had mastered part or all of the curriculum, or had received instruction in the secret lore of the ryu. In most cases, particularly in martial ryu, there was little need for menkyo from a practical perspective. One either had the skills or he did not, and his survival in combat—or lack thereof—was a much better proof of this than any documentation. Menkyo mattered most in establishing the succession of the ryu. The holder of a license granting him the right to carry on the core of the ryu was, de facto, its leader, or at least a teacher qualified by the ryu's leader.

This method of licensing worked well for a feudal ryu. It is still in place today in extant ryu of all kinds. That Kano chose to ignore it and create his own ranking system says much about him. Kano was among the most modern thinking of the Japanese of his generation. He was thoroughly knowledgeable about Western pedagogic principles. He wrote about these principles, and his theories on education are still studied in universities all over the world by aspiring teachers, who may have no knowledge of Kano's judo. So he would have known about reinforcing progress through some tangible sign. Kindergartners get little gold stars; high school students receive the accolades of the honor roll; progress in judo can be rewarded through the presentation of *kyu,* or lower ranks, and later on, through the same presentation of *dan,* a series of more advanced steps. (These comparisons are not meant to belittle the modern dan-i ranking system. It is one that can work efficiently and objectively in situations budo organizations typically find themselves in, with very large numbers of practitioners. It imposes a coherent order that is necessary for groups that may be scattered worldwide. It makes possible interaction between the groups that fosters further growth and maturation. Further, it is misleading in some respects to characterize the kyu-and-dan method of ranking as purely "modern" in the sense of juxtaposing it against the "traditional" menkyo system. In fact, dan and kyu ranks have been awarded in traditional Japanese arts, including music, flower arranging, and the game of go, as far back as the sixteenth century.)

Interestingly, the introduction of Kano's ten-level ranking system did not coincide with the awarding of colored belts. It was not until 1886, three years later, that Kano gave belts as a symbol of rank. It may have been no more than coincidence, but this was at the same time that the Kodokan was pitted against the Yoshin ryu jujutsu school of Hikosuke Totsuka in a contest sponsored by the Tokyo police. Kano's judoka won handily; the reputation of the Kodokan was established and its membership blossomed. Kano may have been motivated to employ distinctively colored belts by the large numbers of students beginning to study judo with him. While he may have recognized his seniors, and they would have known one another, the newer students would have had trouble telling another beginner from a more advanced student. Black belts would have been a way to know that the practitioners wearing them could offer advice or instruction.

The first belts were *kaku-obi,* the stiff silk bands worn with formal kimono. In 1907, the cotton belt was introduced.

While Kano authorized a ten-level ranking system in his judo, he did not adopt any kind of color scheme to be reflected in the belts worn during training. There were in the Kodokan only black and white belts. And so where did the rainbow of hues worn around the waists of judoka and other budoka come from? Details are sketchy, but it's most likely this innovation came from an extraordinary judoka, Mikonosuke Kawaishi. Kawaishi, born in 1899, began his martial arts training in some form of jujutsu. Around the turn of the century, he began studying judo. In 1926, he went to the United States and taught the art, then moved to England to teach briefly there. In 1936, he began teaching judo in Paris, remaining in France until the war. He returned to Japan and ended up in a Manchurian prison at the end of the war, but eventually returned to Paris and continued to teach judo until he died in 1969. Kawaishi was an intrepid innovator in exploring new ways to introduce judo to non-Japanese. Instead of the Japanese names for techniques, for instance, he instituted a numbering system: First outer leg hook, second hip throw, and so on. He experimented with the awarding of different colored belts to indicate his students' progress. The idea caught on and soon spread to judo dojo throughout Europe. By the early 1950s, the concept had worked its way into the judo that was being taught and practiced in the U.S. By the midsixties, judo organizations such as the United States Judo Federation had devised complicated ranking levels that differed for children, teenagers, and adults. That's the way it happened. And so much for the ambitious explanations proffered by those perhaps well meaning but clueless about the white belt fading to darker shades until it becomes black. And so much for the pseudo-esoteric interpretations that white represents original purity and green a beginner's freshness and so on, assigning some attribute to each color. Whatever Kawaishi's intent, there is simply no evidence that colored belts or anything else pigmented have ancient martial sources. Or deep philosophical meanings. True, in Heian-era Japan, varying levels of officials in the imperial palace wore hats or other insignia that differed by color. But Kano never adopted this practice for his judo. It did not come about until judo had gone to Europe. And it requires a considerable stretch of the imagination to conclude that a judo teacher in Paris would have drawn from Japan's eleventh-century court dress as an inspiration for grading his judo students.

The trivia-minded will, of course, wish to know about those belts presented to the very top echelon of judo authorities, the red-and-white striped, the red, and beyond that. Actually, Kano did provide for a couple of these in his ranking system. And in their case, there may be a reasonable argument made that he drew on ancient historical sources. Beginning with the Genpei War (1180–1185), in which the two sides used distinctive battle flags and other paraphernalia—red on the side of the Taira or Heike clan and white for the forces of the Minamoto or Genji family—red and white have figured in Japanese culture. (The two stars in the constellation of

Orion, known in the West as Rigel and Betelgeuse, are known in Japanese astronomical folklore respectively as the *Genji-boshi* and *Heike-boshi,* the former thought to have a reddish hue, the latter white. The two *boshi,* or stars, are thought to represent the families, still struggling to get at one another in the night sky.) *Kohaku,* the combination of red and white, then, has figured prominently in motifs in Japan, including, of course, the two colors of the Japanese national flag. In 1884 Kano supervised the first Red and White Tournament at the Kodokan, a tradition that continues today. For many years, in all judo contests a strip of red cloth was tied around one combatant's belt to make it easier to tell him from his opponent—a method also used in kendo matches. Since 1951, Japan's NHK TV network has sponsored the famous *Kohaku Uta Gassen,* the Red and White Singing Contest, each January. Intramural sports pit red against white teams, and grammar school children often wear red or white hats as a part of their uniforms. And so Kano was drawing on a well-established concept when he created an obi of alternating stripes of red and white that he reserved for sixth, seventh, and eighth dan, ranks that have to do more with the contributions one has made to judo rather than as symbols of technical skill. A solid red belt denotes the status of ninth and tenth dan. There does not seem to have been any provision made for an eleventh dan, so presumably if you make it that far you may feel free to create your own design and color scheme. The twelfth dan was reserved for Kano himself, designated by a white belt twice the width of the original.

Today, judo dojo and organizations have wide latitude in awarding a panoply of colored sashes. For some, the array is viewed as a scheme. More belt ranks imply more testing periods for the dojo; more tests offer the opportunity for the school to charge for them, increasing their profit. Others are dismissive of yellow and blue and purple and green and so on, because they trivialize the art being taught. If one is motivated by a series of belts, how serious can he be? It is worth noting that in most judo dojo in Japan today, all kyu grades wear white belts. (Some dojo may use brown belts for the three highest kyu grades.) There are good arguments to be made on both sides of this issue. Perhaps the best answer might be to accept the system of colored belts as it stands, while realizing simultaneously that outward symbols have little bearing on the inner development that is the goal of all Japanese budo. If one wishes to enter into the realm of these arts, one must make accommodations for their rules and regulations. It is moral preening to decry the ranking structure of a budo while rhapsodizing wistfully about some golden era of the past when the art was above such things. All modern budo incorporated ranking very soon after they emerged as distinct arts; to pretend otherwise is historically fraudulent. It is pretentious to make much ado about one's belt color or rank. It is equally so to hold in disdain a fundamental aspect of the art to which one is allegiant.

And speaking of budo, what of the belts worn in other Japanese combative arts? Kendo never used belts as a part of their training uniforms, although they adopted a dan-i method of grading with the establishment of the All-Japan Kendo Federation in 1928. Aikido copied Kano's innovative dan-i method of grading over a protracted period of time. Ueshiba seems to have been reluctant to initiate it. All of the ranks he gave in his aikido prior to World War II were of the menkyo variety, consistent with classical martial arts. He did not adopt the dan-i system until after the end of the war, and even then he continued to give menkyo licenses along with dan and kyu grades. It was not until the late 1950s that the latter began to be used exclusively in aikido. In 1926, the Okinawan karateka Choki Motobu published a book on his art, illustrated with photos showing him and his students attired in short trousers and bare-chested, but wearing thick black belts around their middles. Two years earlier, Gichin Funakoshi had granted the first shodan black belts to seven of his students. To be sure, a plausible reason for the popularity of the belt system in karate circles in Japan at this time was the same one that encouraged it in judo: it was convenient and made the levels of the practitioners easy to ascertain quickly. However, all forms of Okinawan karate being taught on the mainland of Japan at this time were strongly encouraged to incorporate the dan-i way of assigning ranks for the same reason, mentioned earlier, that they adopted the keikogi: it made them look and seem more "Japanese," an important factor in the acceptance of their arts.

Even more important in the history of karate's use of belts as symbols of rank was the growing power of the Dai Nippon Butokukai, the Great Japan Martial Virtue Society. Founded in 1895 with the backing of several military and governmental leaders in Japan, and with support from the imperial family, the aim of the society ostensibly was to bring ranking and teaching in Japan's many martial arts into some kind of national conformity. (The more cynical among us would note that this occurred at a time when Japan was beginning to flex certain nationalistic tendencies. Exploiting the "virtues" of martial ardor was a neat way of influencing popular opinion and jingoistic attitudes. The even more cynical would observe that the very nature of Japanese martial arts, given their clannish roots and intense sense of loyalty to small groups, is antithetical to big, orderly maintenance. From that perspective, the Butokukai was more a perversion of classical martial values than it was a substantiation of them.) The Butokukai exerted tremendous pressures on Japanese martial arts in the early decades of the twentieth century. They were perceived in many quarters as the "official" budo organization in Japan, and an art could be considered authentic and reputable if it was recognized by the Butokukai. Not surprisingly, nearly all karate groups sought affiliation with the society. Among the demands for this official recognition by the Butokukai was that the art must have a uniform worn by all practitioners and a system that ranked them. (The society also demanded a formal name for the art being presented, which, in the case of one karate group informed of this requirement, resulted in a quick meeting outside the offices of the Butokukai at which a historical ryu name was suddenly "discovered.") For that reason alone, karate leaders implemented the dan-i method by the first part of the twentieth century.

In the fifties and early sixties, Western writers often described the keikogi, when their subject was the mysterious Japanese fighting arts, in words that now seem quaint. Judo experts were attired in "robes" or "kimono." There was no good equivalent for *keikogi* in English. There still is not, but the *karategi*, or just the truncated *gi*, is so well known that novelists now can use it knowing the average reader, even if he has never practiced a budo, knows the term. Ironically, as it has become a common kind of clothing worn outside the Japanese dojo, the question is put to us, do we need to wear it? Starting back in the seventies it was subjected to all sorts of customizing, true. Fabric in colors other than the traditional white was used. Florid patches sprouted on the sleeves and legs. Stylish bell-bottomed trousers, gaudy piping, and, of course, the inevitable displays of ego and advertising, with names and schools emblazoned across the back, all became familiar sights in martial arts training halls. Even with these modifications, however, most practitioners assumed the training uniform was as essential to karate as making a fist correctly, as fundamental to judo or aikido as learning how to take a fall.

Time marches on, though. And the question of uniforms as a necessity or even a salubrious aspect of martial arts training is raised now. The reason for the question in some instances is legitimate and, as might be imagined, mercantile in origin. Proprietors of martial arts schools note that one hurdle many potential customers do not wish to confront is this one: they think they'd look silly in the blousy, pajamalike keikogi. (It is an ironic reversal. When the budo were first promoted outside Japan, part of their élan and attraction was the exotic outfit.)

The proprietors of those schools are absolutely right about this concern. The beginning karateka or aikidoka or judoka, standing about self-consciously in a uniform still starchy-stiff and creased from the packaging folds, his belt incorrectly knotted and askew, does not cut a terribly suave figure. So why not take a cue from fitness studios? Allow leotards, sweatpants, tank tops, and T-shirts. Whatever, within reason, people would feel comfortable in working out or mowing the lawn should be appropriate for learning a fighting art. The argument is supplemented by a commonsense position that "on the street" we are not apt to be attacked while wearing a keikogi, and so we ought to train in the clothes in which we are more likely to meet unexpected violence.

For the vast majority of what passes for budo instruction in this country this argument has a great deal of merit. These places are nothing more than specialized fitness gyms anyway. The atmosphere is similar. There is no sense of a spiritual component present. There is no sense of belonging to a tradition, of following a path as exactly as possible that was laid out by previous generations of exponents. Narcissism permeates. The desire to *look* good is nearly as important as to *feel* good, and both these needs far outweigh any desire for practice as a means of annealing one's spirit to *accomplish* good. This is fine for those who want it, and Lycra and spandex and sweatpants in such a setting are perfectly appropriate. They have no place, however, on the floor of a real dojo.

The person interested in pursuing budo in a serious way begins by recognizing that the Way he is about to enter is different from normal activities. If it were not, why would he bother? Why take up something like the budo if more familiar, cheaper, and more accessible pastimes like softball or an aerobics class would suffice for physical fitness or socializing? No, he knows there is something about these Ways that he wants in his life. That somehow it is special. He may not be sure how it is different. Almost certainly, in fact, the beginner does not. But he knows it's there and he wants it.

The wearing of a keikogi is a physical way of establishing that this activity is not like others. As his training progresses, it is interesting and informative and worthwhile, from time to time, to train in street clothes, just as it is to train outside or in other conditions than can be found in the dojo. But there is something equally as valuable in wearing a keikogi. It is true that beginners look awkward in a new keikogi. (Despite what you might think, they'd look nearly the same no matter what they wear, as soon as they try the basic movements of the art.) They *are* awkward. Part of any budo training is coming face-to-face with this awkwardness, acknowledging it, and then attempting to overcome it.

Being willing to put on a strange uniform is really one of the least uncomfortable challenges faced by the new budoka.

He must also contend with an odd and new terminology. (We will address this in another chapter. Even native speakers of Japanese must deal with this; the vocabulary of the dojo includes dozens of words not used in normal life.) And with modes of behavior that are quite different from those he encounters day-to-day. Yes, there probably are ways of teaching that will avoid any of these discomforts. To take those roads is to wander from the path of the budo, however—make no mistake about it.

Individuals who can gracefully accept discomfort, looking awkward and "uncool," are exactly the sorts that are welcome in a real dojo. There aren't a lot of them around. Not as many, to be sure, as are going to be attracted to exercise gyms. They tend to be of a different sort. To recognize this about oneself is a big step in following a path of the budo. To learn to wear and be comfortable in a training uniform is a sign this step has been taken.

4

THE HAKAMA

"I heard you practiced at the dojo last night," a woman I met the following day gushed. She was nearly incredulous. In the small town in Japan where I was staying, a foreigner was news sufficient to warrant a couple of articles in the regional paper. A foreigner who actually went to the local martial arts training hall and participated in the activities there was, judging by the reactions I'd gotten, something akin to Elvis being resurrected and strolling, in sequined jumpsuit, through a small burg in Mississippi.

"And I heard you wore—" and her eyes widened—"a *hakama!*"

I had had quite enough. For the past several days I had endured, as most foreigners in rural Japan must politely do, accolades of amazement. I could and would eat rice from a bowl. I knew enough to keep the soap out of the public bath when I visited there. I could, in short, display such forms of sophistication as would be thought to be quite beyond the abilities of anyone not blessed to be born Japanese.

"Look," I said, through clenched teeth. "I wear a hakama

six mornings and two evenings a week. I am reasonably sure I own more hakama than any man in your family. It is not unusual," I said, with a certain testiness, "for me to wear a hakama."

Venting such frustrations is not infrequently tempting for the visitor to Japan who has even a passing knowledge of the culture there. One's linguistic skills are praised lavishly for being able to say "Good morning" in a reasonably articulate fashion. After a while there is the sense that you are being treated like a toddler who, after several tries, finally manages a bite of banana slurry that concludes with more in his mouth than on his face. Even so, it does not do to give in to such frustrations too often. It is boorish and ungracious, especially so in the case of my wearing a hakama. Unless they are engaged in specialized activities like the tea ceremony or getting married in a traditional formal ceremony, it is unlikely any Japanese will be wearing a hakama any more often than would a foreigner. And so a certain amount of astonishment about it among Japanese is to be expected. Or at least tolerated. Among those special activities when Japanese would wear hakama today, of course, are some forms of budo. Practitioners of kendo, kyudo, *iaido,* and some forms of aikido all wear hakama, as do most exponents of the classical *koryu bujutsu,* the martial arts of the feudal era that preceded the modern budo forms.

Four hundred years ago, martial arts practice was conducted in hakama not because it was a special kind of "uniform" but because it was a garment most members of the samurai class wore as part of their daily clothing. Where did it come from? One explanation for the development of the hakama was that it was originally a sort of chaps, worn by horsemen in Japan to protect their legs from brush or undergrowth while riding. The leather used by American cowboys for this would have been too precious a commodity in Japan. Rough, thick cotton was used instead to create a heavy kind of apron skirt to meet this sartorial need. Or so goes the explanation. Doubtless the warrior class in feudal Japan did find hakama suitable for protection on horseback. And the image of the samurai out riding the range on his trusty steed is a neat and romantic complement to our own cowboy. The truth is, though, that the origin of hakama-type pants goes back to at least the mid-eighth century, before the samurai emerged as a distinguishable caste. Women of the imperial court during the Heian era (794–1185) wore culottes under their multilayered kimono that were tied very much like hakama. In all likelihood these were the original inspiration for hakama. By the end of the Heian era, men were wearing *kariginu,* or formal hunting attire, and *suikan,* a slightly less formal version of dress, that both featured billowing skirtlike pants. (The first use of the word *hakama* known to be used is *nubakama,* which refers to a specific type of these big-legged pants worn by the nobility when playing *kemari,* a kind of kickball tennis.)

In 1185 the warrior family of the Minamoto defeated the Taira, signaling the end of the Heian period and the beginning of the Kamakura period (1185–1332). The age was named after the city of Kamakura in eastern Japan, which became the political seat of the government and the home of the shogun. Fashion of the day took its cues less from the flowery and lavish Imperial Kyoto court that had dominated during the Heian epoch and more from the quiet, almost severe military sensibilities of the warrior culture of Kamakura. The kariginu and suikan styles of fashion were replaced by the less ostentatious *hitatare,* a standard form of dress for samurai of the Kamakura age. If you have seen any of the formal exhibitions of *yabusame,* or mounted archery, men on horseback galloping along a track and loosing arrows at targets as they go, you have seen hitatare. The upper garment is a loose, kimono-type robe (the tassels hanging from the sleeves are actually drawstrings that could be used to tighten sleeve openings if desired); the pants are very similar to the hakama still worn today. The only significant difference between these older versions and the modern hakama is that the leg openings of the older hakama also had drawstrings and were kept snug, giving the wearer a look something like a character out of *Ali Baba and the Forty Thieves.*

Fans of samurai movies would recognize the *suo* and *daimon,* two variations of the hitatare that evolved during the remainder of the Kamakura period and into the Muromachi era (1340–1570) that followed. These robes differed little from their predecessors save for the materials used to make them. Instead of the luxurious silks of the hitatare, the later versions of the suo and daimon (the latter was the first clothing carrying five family crests that were later used on formal kimono) were made of simple linen, as were the hakama worn with them. The choice of materials was not accidental. The Muromachi age saw the dominance of the military class in Japan. Their quieter, simpler tastes in fabrics for hakama were a reflection of the prevalent societal attitudes and trends of the age.

It wasn't until about 1600, after the shogun Tokugawa Ieyasu unified the country, that the hakama took another step in its evolution. It is difficult to overestimate the momentous changes unification under the Tokugawa regime wrought in Japan. Emerging from a civil war that had lasted for centuries, the shogun was faced with the task of controlling an entire class of military men who, for the most part, had few skills or interests that didn't involve fighting. It is a testament to Ieyasu's genius for ruling that he was able to divert the samurai caste into occupations that, if not always as productive as their former pursuits, were at least less bloody. The samurai of the Tokugawa era was often an engineer overseeing the building of roads and levees, a tax assessor, or a government bureaucrat. During this transitional period, the samurai adapted the old hunting costume, or *kataginu,* of the Heian period, shortening the sleeves and adding stiff, starched "wings" to the shoulders, to create the *kamishimo.* The hakama worn with a kamishimo was so long that the legs had to be bound up when worn outside. Inside, they dragged on the floor several feet behind the wearer, something like a bride's train. Often called a *nagabakama* ("long hakama"), these curious pants look awkward. Walking in them would have required a shuffling step; nobody was going to run in them for long without going facedown.

Several sources suggest the fashion of nagabakama was a deliberate move on the part of the Tokugawa regime. Men wearing such enormous pants would have been restricted in any kind of movement required for combat, goes the explanation, and so nagabakama were encouraged by the authorities to help put a damper on dueling or other martial violence. It's an intriguing notion. If we examine ancient *densho,* or scrolls devoted to the techniques of different ryu, however, we can often see illustrations of men posed in action in these long hakama. Japan's warrior class was nothing if not inventive. They developed methods allowing them to shoot a bow while treading water, wield a sword in a pitch-black room, and use a wood-and-rope lead for a horse as a weapon. So it isn't likely a pair of baggy trousers would have prevented them from figuring out a way to fight. The more probable explanation for the nagabakama's popularity was that Tokugawa Japan saw a renaissance of fashion from the Heian era. The nagabakama, like the bell-bottoms of the sixties that were inspired by nineteenth-century sailor's pants, were more likely an attempt to recapture the elegance of an earlier time. The fact that fighting in them would have been more troublesome was more a fortuitous consequence of fashion than a primary function. Assuming your training hall does not have a problem with spontaneous duels or other such hot-blooded activities, there is no reason to wear your hakama dragging the ground. The correct length, as it was for most of the time when the hakama was a part of everyday clothing in old Japan, is so that the bottom hem comes to just around the anklebone.

By the middle of the Tokugawa period, hakama were worn by the samurai class as well as by merchants and scholars. Incidentally, fans of Japanese period films will recognize a hakama-like garment, one with the legs bound, looking like a sort of pantaloon. These are *momohiki,* worn by lower-class foot soldiers and others not necessarily of the military caste. Two kinds of hakama that are also fashion vestiges of this era are the *tattsuke-bakama* and the *nobakama.* Both are tied at the waist like a regular hakama, but both have narrow legs more like Western-style pants. The nobakama ("field hakama") was a useful garment to wear working out in the fields. The tattsuke-bakama was typically worn with the legs bound up with *kyahan,* or cloth leggings. These are a favorite part of the couture of the cinematic "ninja." They are worn mostly today by *taiko* drummers and by *yobidashi,* the ring attendants at sumo tournaments.

Even after the rapid westernization of Japan after 1868, hakama continued to be formal wear for men and, up until the 1930s and into the Second World War, they were still around as everyday dress for older Japanese men. (Historically, the hakama was worn by women as well as by men, especially during the Kamakura era and later in the nineteenth-century Taisho and Meiji periods.) It was the end of World War II that signaled the eclipse of the hakama as a type of dress that could be seen regularly on Japanese streets. Even if the traditional style could have withstood the onslaught of Western fashion that swept over Japan, postwar shortages on cloth would have made the hakama too costly to have been produced. More than one of Ueshiba Morihei's early aikido students has recalled having to borrow hakama from older relatives for training—leading to some consternation on the part of the owners, since the hakama were of the expensive silk variety and didn't hold up well under the rigors of training. Today, men may still dress in formal kimono and hakama for certain events deemed appropriate for such wear: at formal ceremonies for retiring sumotori, for instance, as well as at traditional weddings. But certainly by the end of World War II, the hakama as an item of daily fashion was entirely gone in Japan. The only remnant of it as a regularly worn item of clothing is in those martial arts dojo where it is a standard part of the dress.

The hakama worn in today's dojo are, to be technical, *joba hakama,* a version with the legs separated. (*Joba* means "horse-riding." The separation of the legs made straddling a horse easier.) Some formal hakama are actually skirts without separate legs, but these are not used in any kind of budo training. A typical hakama has four pleats on the right leg and three on the left. Like nature's reaction to a vacuum, it is a characteristic of the human imagination that, where a space exists, we find something to fill it in. Such is the case with the "reason" for the pleats, the number of which, if we are to believe stories that go around, represent seven virtues of the noble warrior—courage, fidelity, honor, good hygiene, plays well with others—I don't know. I do know there is no evidence of this in any historical Japanese texts on clothing I have seen. I have never heard of this explanation at all, in fact, outside Western dojo or books that purport it to be so. I suspect it is fantasy or, at best, an ambitious bit of back-formation. A more reasonable explanation has been advanced: the right leg, with fewer pleats and therefore less "blousy," would be easier to move, and so getting up or sitting down, assuming the right leg moved first. The right leg *did* normally move first, in no small part because the sword has always been worn on the left hip and standing on the right leg first meant one was less vulnerable to a surprise attack.

There is one pleat in the rear of the hakama. (Maybe, if we buy into the virtues supposedly represented by these folds, it represents the better part of valor, as it does facilitate the ability to swiftly run away.) Inside that pleat, up at the top of the garment, is a little spoon-shaped toggle. It is a *hera,* Japanese for "spatula," since it is similarly shaped. The hera is meant to be tucked into the back of the belt to help keep the waist of the hakama in place and to facilitate in hoisting the rear of the skirt just a little. In the formal silk hakama I have inherited from my teacher and from his teachers, the toggles are carved of ivory and are probably worth almost as much as the garment itself. Today's hakama hera are more likely to be made of plastic.

The hard flat plate at the hakama's rear waist is the *koshi-ita,* or "hip-board." A fixture of Hong Kong kung-fu movies of the late sixties was the Japanese villain who was inevitably dressed in kimono and hakama—and almost as inevitably the hakama would be worn backward, so the koshi-ita was over the belly. A least one notorious martial arts "master," one in New York City back in the early seventies, wore a hakama backward and claimed the plate was a form of abdominal protection. Those purporting to be experts in the budo in those days were not always well informed, but they were creative. In any case, the koshi-ita belongs behind you and not in front. And if you see a hakama without one, it is probably meant to be worn by a female practitioner of kyudo. Because women have traditionally worn their hakama higher around the waist than men, the koshi-ita was dispensed with in women's hakama sometimes. Kyudo has continued this style.

A hakama is almost always worn along with a soft cloth belt underneath and wrapped around the wearer's waist. (Kendo is an exception. The hakama is tied on directly over the jacket. The *tare,* or hip protector, and *do,* the torso armor, help keep the hakama in place for the kendoka.) Aikido practitioners who wear hakama usually opt to wear the comparatively narrow cloth belt worn by those in judo or karate dojo, knotting it in front. Other practitioners use a more traditional wide obi that's circled about the waist a few times, then tied with a flat knot in the rear, right above the hips. The knot at the rear serves the purpose of acting as a kind of small bustle that pulls the back of the hakama hem up just enough to help prevent one's heels from catching on it while walking, keeping it from dragging on the floor or ground. Some aikidoka take exception to this, insisting *they* wear their knot in the front and *they* don't trip on the hem or dirty it. To which I would respond, "How often do *you* practice outside or on uneven ground or anyplace other than in the confines of a perfectly flat and smooth matted dojo floor?" They will then insist that the knot in the rear can be potentially harmful and at the least painful if one falls directly onto his back while training. To which I would respond that "you do not know how to tie a proper knot." These arguments on both sides aside, the wise student will follow the conventions of his dojo. But all practitioners whose training includes the wearing of a hakama should know how to tie a knot at the rear simply because of the history of the garment. Formally worn, a hakama always has a wide belt underneath, always knotted at the rear.

Speaking of knots and of formality, some martial artists who wear hakama use the *ju-musubi* or *juji-shime,* the "figure-ten knot" when tying up the cords of their hakama. The name derives from the cross shape of the knot, resembling the written character for the numeral ten in Japanese. This is a formal way of knotting the hakama as it is used for tea ceremony or other similar occasions. Worn in the dojo, unless for some special event, the knot looks pretentious. While it may seem odd that something like a knot could have connotations of pretension, the variety of tying things together in Japanese culture can convey a great deal of significance. Imagine, to get some idea of it, how strange it would look to wrap garbage in an old newspaper and then tie the package up with an elaborate bow of the sort used for a birthday present. The cords of the hakama worn for daily, regular training in the dojo should be tied in a simple square or reef knot, the dangling ends tucked back into the waist neatly. There is a tale passed on in some dojo that the left end should be tucked up under the belt, the right should go in the opposite direction, over the belt, because this represents the duality of *in-yo* (yin-yang), hard-soft, and so on. OK. Maybe. Sounds a lot like the "hakama pleats represent . . ." stuff to me. In practical terms, if your art involves wearing a sword or having a *bokken* taken in and out of the belt as though you were drawing a real weapon, putting the right cord over the top of the belt will lessen chances of it coming out during practice.

The vents at the sides of the hakama are called *soba*, literally the "side view." Another word pronounced the same way but written with different kanji refers to a kind of noodles. It is material for some good puns. Suffice it to say that where hakama soba are concerned, it is déclassé to stand around with your hands stuck through the vents as though they were pockets. The origination of this notion is probably because a person standing about with his hands so concealed could have been holding a weapon with them and so others were understandably uncomfortable with it. In some periods of the hakama's development, the soba slits extended far down to below the knees. Formal hakama will still have a longer and wider soba than those used in the dojo. When doing chores around the dojo, you can tuck up some of the material in the legs into the vents of your hakama to keep your legs free. In the old days—and in samurai movies—the sight of a man tucking his hakama legs up meant that he was getting ready to do serious battle (or at least something serious). The act was rather like the cowboy pushing his jacket out of the way of his holstered gun before going into the shoot-out. Tucking up one's hakama legs was called *momodachi,* an obviously archaic term I was quite proud of knowing when I was younger and which I once confused, while speaking with several older Japanese, with *momo-iroyugi,* which means literally "peach-colored," but which is a similarly old-fashioned euphemism for "foreplay."

Folding a hakama after it's been taken off following a training session should be a daily part of your activities in the dojo. It folds into a small, neat square, the cords laced together in a knot, so it will not be wrinkled when packed into a bag. Folding a hakama is a skill best taught to a junior by his seniors in the dojo. It is not particularly difficult, even though it may look intimidating, dealing with all those pleats and cords. Practice makes it almost automatic; the process serves as a pleasant sort of ritual that concludes the training session, and it leaves the hakama folded without unnecessary creases.

The earliest hakama material was a simple cloth woven from fibers of *kuzu,* or arrowroot plant. Up until the Edo period, a variation of this rough but light cloth, called *kakko,* was popular for making hakama worn during the hot summer months. Formal hakama made of a silk called *sendai hira* came along about four centuries ago, a technological improvement on an earlier method of silk weaving from Kyoto called *nishijin.* Sendai hira is a lustrous silk textile with a soft sheen that does not wrinkle easily and is comfortable to wear. Hakama made of it are enormously expensive garments and fortunately not appropriate for budo except for very formal exhibitions or demonstrations. Hakama for the dojo are something of a retro fashion, harkening back to the era of the earlier and simpler plant-fiber materials. Once cotton became widely available in Japan, hakama worn for budo were made of it. Today, blends and synthetic materials are all available. Some of these hold their creases better than others. If you are practicing in an aikido dojo that places a lot of emphasis on kneeling techniques, you will want to consider a heavier grade of fabric to keep the knees of the garment intact as long as possible. If your training is often conducted outside, you may want to go with an all-cotton version, since it will take repeated washings more easily than some other fabrics.

Hakama sabaki is the skill of walking, training, and sitting while wearing a hakama. It can be a little trickier than it might first seem. If there are aikidoka or *iaidoka* who have worn hakama very long at all who tell you they have never tripped over a hem in the middle of their practice, they are either remarkably graceful or mendacious. The method of walking successfully in a hakama, of moving around quickly and gracefully, requires some practice. *Gaki-daisho* is an archaic expression for the kind of arrogant swaggering done by a fellow carrying a pair of swords. The late actor Toshiro Mifune often adopted this strut when he played samurai in movies, the legs of his hakama swinging wide with each step. Real samurai were admired for walking *shizo-shizo,* or quietly, with the knees just slightly bent, so their hakama did not move much at all. Walking in hakama, particularly outside, can be a test of skill, especially in wet weather while wearing zori slippers. Either zori or some other type of sandal or toothed clog geta were the only footwear premodern Japanese had. They invariably flipped mud or water up along the back of the wearer if he wasn't careful. It's a worthwhile experience if you have the chance: walk across a wet lawn wearing your zori and hakama, then take the skirt off and have a look to see if the back is dry.

When sitting on the floor, there are some tricks that can keep the wide legs of the hakama from getting wadded up under your legs. One is from the Ogaswara ryu, a school of etiquette that created rules and manners for the warrior class and which is discussed in greater detail in the chapter on bowing. It calls for lightly swishing the left and right legs of the hakama behind the knees just before sitting, making the material from the legs flare out to the sides like the wings of a bird after one is seated. (*Lightly* is the operative word here. Ostentatiously slapping the legs with a distinct *pop* is boorish, according to the protocols of the Ogaswara ryu.) The wearer brushes the inside of his left leg first as he begins to kneel, then the right. Done correctly—it requires some practice to look and feel natural—the legs of the hakama will fall to the floor so they don't get wrapped around your legs when you try to get up. In the etiquette of the tea ceremony, there are a couple of variations on this. In one method, both hands are lightly pressed against the thighs as one kneels, sliding down the length of the legs until just before the knees touch the floor, when they brush the front of both hakama legs to the sides. In another, both hands brush back the hakama legs at the inside of the knees simultaneously as one kneels. These variants reflect different schools of etiquette in old Japan, some of which had influences over tea ceremony ryu.

Who wears a hakama in the dojo? In most classical koryu, the hakama is worn from the moment one begins training. The same is true for iaido, kyudo, and *naginata-do*. Aikido seems to be the only budo form where hakama-wearing is some kind of privilege or proof of rank. Why this has evolved within aikido is a mystery. Demonstrably, it was not always so. Most early photos of aikido training (ca. 1930) have practitioners all in hakama. It was not until some time after the end of World War II that hakama in aikido dojo were linked to rank. One possible explanation is that with the rapid growth of the art, teachers needed a quick way to recognize beginners, and so hakama were reserved for those who had achieved dan status. A more likely scenario has been suggested by more than one early postwar student of the art: Fabric of any kind was extremely rare in Japan after its defeat by the Allies. While Ueshiba may have been a stickler for the formality implied by wearing a hakama in class, circumstances probably dictated that the majority of his students could not have afforded the garment. And so, the practice became, "well, only advanced students *need* to wear hakama." If this is so, it is ironic that the traditions of the aikido dojo have turned that on its head and now it is only those advanced students who "get" to wear the skirt. Another anomaly of the hakama in aikido has been its use among women. While men are often prohibited from wearing one before they attain the required rank, female students of aikido wear the skirt as soon as they start their training. Why? The "official" explanation has to do with feminine modesty. Apparently some mid-twentieth-century aikido teachers felt women in pants were risqué. And so down went the edict that women should be attired in hakama regardless of rank. One need know only the rudiments of recent social history to imagine how well this has been received by modern women.

Most practitioners of koryu arts do not wear pants under their hakama, while most practitioners of aikido do. There is an explanation—this one is often trotted out with the subject, just mentioned above, of women wearing hakama in the aikido dojo—that pants were originally underwear worn below the hakama, and so the practice of covering them is traditional and modest. It would not do to have women training in what was, essentially, underwear. Nope. Nothing like modern pants existed in premodern Japan, as we noted in the previous chapter on the keikogi. The habit of wearing pants beneath one's skirt may have arisen because of *suwari-waza*, the techniques of aikido that are practiced while crouching on one's knees. The extra layer of cloth between the knees and the mat can provide some protection against abrasions and burns. Since some of Ueshiba's first students came from judo, which had more recently adopted long pants as part of its uniform, they may have made this an accepted part of the aikido training outfit. If you do wear pants under your hakama, take special care to see that the bottom of the pant legs do not extend out below the hem of the hakama. It's a fashion faux pas. Of course, there are faux pas and then there is the gauche. Wearing a belt as a display of rank *outside* the hakama is among the latter. Some classical martial arts schools might do this, to simulate a sash from which a long sword was hung, or to make it easier to slide a wooden practice sword in and out of the place it would have been worn, or even to use as a grip for opponents in practicing grappling techniques. Still, worn wrapped around the waist outside the hakama, a belt gives the distinct impression one cannot resist the temptation to display one's rank—even at the risk of looking like a boob to do so.

When considering the whole role of the hakama in the budo dojo or anywhere else, one is reminded of an adage usually applied to Japanese kimono: "Kae nai, kirare nai, tatame nai" (Can't afford to buy, can't wear correctly, can't fold). The average Japanese male, climbing into a hakama for his wedding or some other event (there are even hakama made now with Velcro fasteners to mimic the look of the real knot), tends to regard it much the same way a typical American male reacts to his rented dinner jacket. Both the Japanese and the American might prefer their respective formal dress over, say, porcupine-quills underwear. But not by much. Those of us in Japan and elsewhere who spend much of our time wearing this odd skirt should learn to do so correctly. But we must be tolerant of those who wonder at a choice of clothing that, to be quite honest, is probably a good sign we're a bit odd ourselves.

5

WEAPONS

BUKI

The evening's middle hours. An interlude. The commuter mobs surging out of businesses and offices all over Tokyo, packed into the trains with breathtaking density, have finally slowed to a trickle. It is still too early for the late-night revelers to come aboard and, if you are riding on most of the train lines around the city, you can get a seat—even most of a whole car—to yourself. The four of us had done just that, on the Tozai Blue Line out of the Nihonbashi station. One of our car was a girl in her twenties, a *chajin,* a student of the tea ceremony, perched on the edge of the seat with gentle poise in a blue and white patterned kimono. A few seats away was a kendoka, sitting erect, fists on his thighs, alert. Beside him a *shokunin* leaned back, arms folded comfortably across his midriff, dozing after what must have been a long day laboring as a woodworker.

Any good Sherlock could have pointed out to his Dr. Watson the clues to the identities of my fellow passengers. Not many young women wear kimono nowadays, for instance. Not unless they're involved in a traditional art like the tea ceremony. The shokunin had the broad, leathery fingers of a man who chisels and hammers for more than a hobby—for more than just a living, either. His callused hands were those of a craftsman who builds because it is what he loves. The collegiate kendoka? He had the wiry physique and steely eyes of a martial artist, a twentieth-century swordsman. But the real giveaways to their various backgrounds were what they each carried. The tools beside them marked them as surely as fingerprints, tools that in Japanese are called *dogu:* instruments of the Way.

Cultures, civilizations with even the most primitive tools at their command, inevitably afford some respect to these objects. The Stone Age fletcher who knapped out a flint projectile point felt, no doubt, something beyond just technical satisfaction for the weapon he'd made that protected him or brought down his food. Tools are not, by their definition, works of art in the true sense of the word. Yet neither can the well-made, well-used tool ever be considered purely utilitarian. The tools of Japan's traditional arts and Ways are evocative examples of this attitude, one that expresses a sense about the tool that places it in our estimation—some of us anyway—as an object between a practical instrument and an art object. Tools in premodern Japan were used to create, just as they are everywhere. Dogu in Japan as well have long been considered capable of elevating the spirit of their users. And so the relationship between the artisan and his tools transcended mere craft. Dogu provided the vehicle (they still do) to travel a philosophical, potentially transformational, path.

To recognize this aspect of the Japanese dogu is to understand their essence. To appreciate it as it applies to the "tools" of the martial artist is to grasp a fundamental concept of his art.

Except for some advanced kata that involve the use of a mock dagger and wooden sword, judo does not normally use any kind of *buki,* or weapons, in its practice. Other budo do, however, and they are a constant presence in most dojo. Aikido uses daggers, swords, and staffs. Kendo, of course, uses bamboo "swords," along with wooden swords or metal ones (called *shinken* if they have a sharp blade and *mogito* or *iaito* if the blade is deliberately dulled for safer practice), which are used for the exercise of kata. In arts devoted to the use of the long-handled glaive or halberd, called a *naginata,* or wooden replicas, some with split bamboo where the sharp convex cutting edge of the weapon would be, are employed. Sticks, ranging from long staffs of about six feet, called *bo,* down to smaller *jo,* which are about four feet in length, down to still shorter *hanbo* or *tanjo*—all are included in various forms of budo training. Karate-do often borrows from the extensive weaponry of Okinawa. The budoka will quickly become accustomed to seeing some or all of these around the dojo.

The majority of weapons are "practice" models, made of wood, usually white oak. To think of them as merely safe substitutes for practice, however, is a mistake. Wooden swords, called bokken or *bokuto,* were used in dueling during Japan's feudal age and have, in skilled hands, caused serious injury and death. In any event, weapons in the dojo should always be treated as "real" in every sense of the word and afforded respect. The history of these wooden weapons is probably not much younger than the real ones they represent, and in fact the wood ones may have well preceded the metal versions. In the case of the sword, proto-historical clublike swords made of stone represent the earliest incarnation of buki in Japan, though one wonders about the practicability of their use. More efficient swords were introduced to Japan from China or elsewhere on the Asian mainland, along with the details of metallurgy necessary for forging them. Yet given the abundance of hardwoods in Japan, early warriors must have experimented with wooden swords that duplicated metal weapons, particularly after the distinctive curvature of the Japanese sword became predominant sometime after the sixth century.

A bokuto, or wooden sword, could not cut, of course. But its blunt blade was monstrously effective at crushing bone. Even a light strike could debilitate or permanently cripple, stun, or kill. Further, with a solid wooden blade the user had little worry about the chipping or breaking, either along the edge or at the point (where the blade was inserted into a hilt), to which a comparatively thinner metal one was subject in the violence of combat. Even if the warrior preferred sharpened steel in his hand in a battle, the bokuto readily found a place in his training. Again, it would be a stretch to think of it as a "safe" alternative. It was, though, *safer*. Almost as important, a wooden sword withstood the rigors of training exercises better than a steel sword and was, when it splintered or cracked, easier to replace.

Virtually all classical martial arts used the bokuto in their practice. Most of them preferred specific models, with a length, weight, or size that was best suited to the techniques of the ryu. Some, like the Jigen ryu of Kyushu, use a heavy bokuto. It works not only as a method of practice but as something of a piece of weight training equipment as well. At the extreme range of the bokuto-as-weight is the *suburito*. These are large, very heavy bokuto that are often manipulated during solo practice, cutting the air, the resistance of their weight working as a device to build stamina and encourage the proper use of muscles in stopping the sword exactly as it should be. Other schools of swordsmanship, like the Shinkage ryu, call for wooden swords that are much, much lighter than any real sword. Their aim with this sort of bokuto is to teach the timing particular to the ryu. Some systems insist on a heavy leather hand guard just where the metal *tsuba,* or guard, would be on a metal sword. (The best leather for this comes from a species of water buffalo not native to Japan and becoming rare in its range in southeast Asia. At the turn of the last century, Japan placed a near-ban on importation of these hides. Now pigskin or other kinds of leather are used, though there is much grumbling that they are not as good as the original buffalo-hide models. Indeed, these thicker and tougher guards, when they are still available, now commonly fetch a much higher price at martial arts supply shops than the bokuto to which they are attached.) Other schools eschew any guard at all, for various reasons. It might, in fact, be possible to make some educated observations about the technical nature of the ryu by looking at the bokuto or other weapons used in its practice.

Almost as well known as the bokuto is the *shinai*, the principal dogu in the art of kendo. The history of the shinai goes back to fairly early in the feudal era, before the first part of the sixteenth century at least. Two very old schools of the sword, the Maniwa Nen ryu and the Shinkage ryu, independently developed shinai. These were sections of bamboo approximately the same length as the swords preferred by these ryu, split longitudinally into four or eight pieces and then bound, either with a rough cloth in the case of the Nen ryu, or with the leather used to encase the shinai of the Shinkage ryu. (These are *fukuro shinai*, or "shinai in a bag.") It was not until the middle of the eighteenth century that the shinai took another step in its evolution. At this time, classical martial systems of swordsmanship had, in some cases, been transmuted into a more modern form that appealed to the masses and which can be classified as the first version of kendo as it exists currently. With thousands of practitioners, few of them from a hereditary warrior class and so without the mentality or background to confront the dangers of training with a bokuto, a safer weapon was needed. Nakanishi Chuto, who lived in the mid-1700s and was a master of the Ono-ha Itto ryu of swordsmanship, provided this. He eventually founded his own school, the Nakanishi-ha Itto ryu, which featured techniques and strategies that looked much like modern kendo. He used a version of the fukuro shinai, adding as well in his dojo thick, cloth-padded *kote,* or gloves, to protect his students' hands against attacks there.

Sometimes overlooked, incidentally, in histories of kendo that laud Nakanishi for these innovations, is the fact that some of his students were disgusted with these safety measures. They regarded them as contrary to the spirit of budo, a compromise that would degrade the art. In a way, this set the stage for a controversy that continues today. Budo forms have always been divided between those on the one hand who believe making training safer and more accessible, with the addition of armor, padding, or substitute weapons, and those on the other hand who wish to maintain a "pure" form of the art. (Of course, there is some question as to what constitutes this purity.) Both sides have fair arguments. If I do not fear having my wrist broken or my skull caved in by your weapon—and similarly if I don't have to worry about injuring you—I am freer to explore the possibilities and execution of techniques I am learning in training. We do not have to be concerned with artificially "pulling" our strikes. We gain confidence knowing that if we have dodged or blocked or successfully maneuvered against an attack, it wasn't just because our partner allowed it, since he was able to make it fully and completely. We had to deal with it honestly and realistically. On the other hand, if I am not concerned about the possibility of being hurt by you when I attack, I can be cavalier about that attack. Sure, you bopped me on my padded wrist or your weapon skimmed alongside my head as I moved in to strike you, but I barely felt it. And if it is a judged contest, the referee will overlook your accidental touch and award me the point. This kind of careless attitude is obviously antithetical to the real spirit of combat implied by serious budo, however. Had the sword been real, those "accidental" brushes would have resulted in an instant amputation of my hand, my carotid artery severed in an eyeblink. Indeed, one has only to look at the sad spectacle of too much modern kendo, with its careless postures and frantic, ill-conceived attacks to see what happens when the element of danger is effectively removed. Further (goes the argument against these innovations), it is impossible to pad the real targets against which the real sword works most effectively: thumbs, arteries in the groin, and under the arms. These are not covered by armor. So the kendoka develops a warped sense of swordsmanship by continually launching strikes against the forehead and torso and other points that would never have been available to an enemy wearing armor on the battlefield.

While this discussion finds merits and points on both sides, it is undeniable that once Nakanishi and others began their experiments with such changes, the die was cast. By the last part of the eighteenth century, Nakanishi had added a padded apron, or tare, to protect the thighs and groin and a *men,* the headgear with its steel ribs that prevented damage to the face. Simultaneously, he tinkered with the shinai, adding even more splits to the bamboo to make the weapon more flexible, and then eventually reducing that number and rounding off the edges of the bamboo to achieve a lighter and more aerodynamic compromise. He got rid of the bag and held the pieces together with strips of leather and added a round hide guard. Nakanishi also standardized to some extent the length of the shinai at about thirty-nine inches. Hitherto, there was no consistency, and participants showed up at early kendo halls with shinai six feet long or longer. (In the twentieth century, kendo authorities in Japan further clarified these lengths, specifying maximum ones for children, students, and adults.) In the 1970s, still another step was taken in the development of the shinai, when they began to be manufactured of carbon and graphite and polymers that replaced the bamboo entirely. Virtually indestructible, these shinai are expensive and, while some traditionalists within the kendo world want nothing to do with them, they are becoming more popular. Their presence is, given the history of the shinai, hardly an insult to "the old ways." They are more accurately just another chapter in the development of kendo that began so many years ago with Nakanishi and will probably continue on.

The other most common wooden weapon found in today's dojo is the jo, or staff. Stick weapons of this size have a long history in Japan's combative arts. The jo owes the impetus of its development to Muso Gonnosuke Katsuyoshi, born sometime in the last quarter of the sixteenth century. Muso was an expert in at least a couple of schools of martial art. His specialty was in the long staff, or bo. (Two different kanji are used to distinguish between the bo and the jo. The best way to think of it is that a bo is usually at least six feet long. A jo is shorter, usually around four feet. Also, the word *bo* refers to a wooden staff or stick. Therefore, the irritating neologism one constantly hears from nonnative Japanese speakers, "bo-staff," is as redundant as saying "mister-man.") Muso was successful in a number of duels until he met the famous swordsman Miyamoto Musashi and challenged him. Musashi defeated Muso, using only a piece of wood he was carving on at the time. Chagrined, Muso retreated to a mountaintop for ascetic training in his art. He was rewarded by a vision that led him to shorten his staff. The result was the foundation of a ryu for the jo that continues today. Other schools and arts used variations of this short stick. In some, it is meant as a sort of emergency weapon, one in the practitioner's hands suddenly when his longer staff or spear was broken in combat. In others, it is concealed, more or less, as a kind of walking stick. In aikido, the jo is primarily used as a medium to illustrate, practice, and refine the elements of the art. It is a supplemental means of training meant to strengthen one's abilities in the empty-hand techniques that are the basis of aikido.

No matter what the particular form of the weapon—and in mentioning the bokuto, shinai, and jo, we are noting only the common ones; there are dozens of them—they are customarily held on racks or *kake* along the walls of the dojo. Outside Japan, these racks are sometimes placed on the shomen, or front wall. They should not be. As we've discussed in the chapter on the kamidana, the front wall of a dojo is a special place; it should not be cluttered and there should not be students coming and going from that area, getting or replacing weapons they use during their class. Instead, these racks should be located along the side or back wall of the dojo. In some dojo, there are rules about the specific placement of the weapons. These vary, and the reasons for them vary as well. In some places, the part of the weapon that is grasped is placed closest to where members enter or approach the racks. The reason given is that it is convenient for this arrangement. In others, the rule will be the opposite. The grip of the sword or other weapon will be placed away from its easiest grasp and the reason will be that historically, during Japan's civil wars, one did not want an intruder to have quick access to a weapon upon entering the dojo. Watch what is the custom in your dojo and follow it. And don't worry too much about anyone bursting in and creating havoc with a seized weapon. It is not a common occurrence in dojo these days.

If they are not on the racks, weapons are laid on the floor along the walls of the dojo, to keep them out of the way or to avoid having someone step on them. This seems to be common sense. But if one is using a weapon and isn't careful, it gets laid on the floor while the teacher pauses the class to explain something or while one is shifting roles between attacker and defender, and sooner or later someone stumbles over it. When they are placed at the edge of the floor or training area, be sure to put them down so the tip, if they are bladed, faces away from the front of the dojo.

Most of the time, each student will supply his own weapons. They should be considered "his," and should not be touched or used without his permission. One explanation for this is that the sword was the "soul of the samurai" and was regarded as an extension of his persona, and so bokuto and other training weapons must be treated as an extension of the owner's persona or as near-sacred regalia. There are some dojo, well-meaning maybe, but pretentious in their application nonetheless, that have complex rituals about approaching the weapons rack, about performing a formal salutation to it, and so on. This is largely romantic nonsense. Swords were tools. They were, just as chisels and saws were for the carpenter, the dogu of the trade for the samurai. Arguably, they were critically important ones, since the lives of their owners depended on their weapons. Just as a modern soldier would not want someone handling his rifle, the samurai wanted to be sure that his weapon was in good and usable condition, and he could do that best by assuring that he was the only one who touched it. His concerns in this regard were more practical than spiritual. However, it is also important to acknowledge that Japan has a long history of affording a special quality to dogu of any sort and this was accentuated in the case of weapons.

During Japan's long feudal period, a samurai walking down a crowded street could be confronted instantly for allowing the scabbard of the sword he wore to clack against that of another warrior's weapon. Touching a sword or any other weapon without permission was a serious breach of etiquette. And it is true that there were prescribed mannerisms and behaviors when handling one's own sword that might seem a bit excessive to us. When a samurai cleaned and oiled his weapon, for instance, he might keep a square of paper between his teeth so the moisture in his breath would not dampen the blade even slightly, risking a threat of rust. And so to place the matter of weapons in the dojo into some perspective, we have to appreciate the balance between the practical and the spiritual qualities they represent. Why this is so in the history of the budo, and how it is distinguished to some degree from prevalent attitudes about tools in general in the West, is interesting.

Plotted on a timeline, there is no single moment to be pinpointed, but somewhere during the nineteenth-century era of the industrial revolution, the concept of the tool as an aesthetic object all but disappeared in the West. Turned out en masse on factory assembly lines, everything from hammers to writing pens lost their individuality. They lost the personalized uniqueness they once had when made individually, often by the owner or with his special needs in mind. Those who owned and used them lost as well a sense of feel and affection for their tools. The American frontiersman, for instance, regarded his flintlock rifle in a way his grandson who worked the coal mines of Pennsylvania could never feel about his pickaxe. In Japan, to a considerable extent, this transition from a dogu, with the special connotation that word implies (literally *dogu* translates to "an implement for the Way"), to a mere utilitarian instrument, did not happen until modern times. That is because Japan did not experience the widespread changes wrought by the industrial revolution until after the Second World War. Additionally, "feudal Japan" was, among other things, a two-century period of celebration of the artist and the craftsman, and so tools were afforded a place within the culture that was not universal in all parts of the world. This applied naturally to the dogu, the tools of the warrior.

Bereft of mass-manufacturing processes that might have stripped them of individual qualities, and with a population that was largely rural and so had a constant and varied need for them, Japanese tools remained for centuries handmade products. The dogu represented a sturdy bridge between art and implement, between the aesthetic and the utilitarian. The Japanese responded to this link by investing sentiments into these usually quite ordinary objects that reveal an element of Japanese culture most extraordinary. Not surprisingly, this sentiment was dramatically evident in the weapons of the samurai class. From the very earliest period of sword-forging in Japan, an element of the religious and spiritual was attached to the process. The smithy is invariably fixed with a Shinto kamidana exactly of the sort described here in the chapter on it. Smiths continue to undergo ablutions and make prayers before work. There is, in their manufacture, something of the mystical in some cases. But even if we dismiss apocryphal tales and superstitions and pseudo-magical claims, we must be cognizant of the role played by swords and other weapons, and we must be aware that this role was not entirely utilitarian.

The presence of weapons in a dojo should give a sobering

awareness to the danger that is inherent in all budo. It does not matter if they have sharp edges or are simply wooden versions. Tap your forefinger sharply on a tabletop: it does not hurt and unless you have some mysterious "death touch" powers, it will not unduly cause grievous harm to another. But think for a moment about what a strike with that same light force would do to your wrist or thumb if it was applied with, for example, a three-foot stick. Weapons increase the force and velocity of movements enormously. Even when training without them, the budo can be dangerous. When they are added to training, one must be constantly vigilant and always consider them capable of doing serious damage. Today, most budoka aren't quite so meticulous as the samurai of old in their regard for their buki. But they should continue to treat their weapons with considerable care and, if they are serious about their art, it is natural that they will imbue those weapons with qualities far beyond those of ordinary objects. It may be partly superstition, partly a sense of aesthetics, and yes, partly spiritual. In any case, it applies to weapons in the dojo and the tradition should be respected.

6

THE SHINTO SHRINE

KAMIDAMA

The beginner enters the dojo for the first time often with the belief that he has embarked on a direction in his life that, while new in some minor ways, will essentially be along the same compass points as previous journeys he's taken. There will be some unfamiliar encounters, he suspects. This is, after all, a Japanese art and there are few cultures more exotic or strange from a Western perspective than that of Japan. But come on. Basically it's a physical activity. You go to a place designated for it, you don the accepted outfit, you warm up, and you participate. Then shower and go home. You develop friendships within the activity and gradually, you hope, you become more skilled at it. Except for the fact you can't drink beer while doing it and you save the cost of a ball, it isn't all that different from joining a bowling league, right? That attitude survives, if it is a serious and traditional dojo into which you have wandered, for about ten minutes. Just long enough for the teacher to clap his hands or one of the seniors to suddenly find a place and have others follow along to line up beside him, and suddenly all are kneeling and there is some more clapping and bowing in the direction of a small, not terribly well decorated doll house sitting unobtrusively on a shelf. And the beginner is left wondering if, rather than a martial arts training hall, he has not come across some kind of cult, and if he will soon be expected to shave his head and begin soliciting funds on street corners. It's not that extreme. But if it is a real dojo and a traditional budo is being taught and practiced there, there is a likelihood the student will soon come to a confrontation, perhaps his first, with Shinto. And then he should, if he has not already, arrive at a realization: there is some stuff going on here that the average softball player or weekend canoeist isn't going to have to deal with in his choice of avocations.

It is beyond the scope of our intent here to discuss the relationship between Shinto and the budo of Japan. And certainly it is beyond me to try to explain Shinto as a religion and as a structure of folk beliefs inherent in Japanese civilization. So as briefly as possible:

Water flows—*nagare* in Japanese—ineluctably. Sometimes the flow is powerful and surging, sometimes in currents and eddies so slow as to seem still. It trickles, gurgles, and splashes and roars. But wherever gravity is at work, water will be flowing on. At its essence, Shinto is a way of looking at life in terms of nagare—flowing. With rhythms not all that different from the flow of water, life moves on, sometimes quickly, other times with agonizing slowness, but always in motion. The degree to which we are aware of the flow, our ability to ride along with it: these are the unifying impulses of Shinto. At its heart is the concept that life flows and that change, renewal, decay, resting, and growing are all natural parts of the cadence of things here on earth. So we may as well adjust to them and appreciate them—endure them when necessary—and always be mindful of from where it is they have emanated and where, eventually, they are bound to lead. There is, then, within the spirit of Shinto, a sense of timelessness. Our ancestors and our posterity are all in the same current along with us. Though they are not present physically perhaps, they are a part of our world. The contributions of the past, the potential of the future; without an awareness of these we become hopelessly self-centered. Properly, we practice our art for ourselves, but also because our teachers have been kind enough to pass it along to us, and so, in some small way, we have an obligation to polish and perfect it. It is our duty to keep the art whole to be passed down to the next generation. And we have debts that should properly be discharged to the generations that have preceded us. These debts are a way of reminding ourselves what we owe those generations and the sacrifices they have made to bring the art to us. That's why Shinto can be described as a form of ancestor worship, which it is. However, along with the reverence for the past is that cognizance of those who will come after us. A constant stream of generations flowing, and where one begins and another ends is never entirely clear, for our ancestors continue to exert a presence in our lives, just as do those who will come in the future.

There are those who argue convincingly that Shinto is not

a religion at all but rather an accretion of various folk beliefs, many of them primeval. This may be so. (However, there are volumes and volumes of ritual and theology pertaining to Shinto, and one suspects, as is sometimes the case with Zen, that such pronouncements are rendered by those who wish to believe that Shinto is somehow beyond the mundane categorization by which other religions are explained and understood.) Certainly Shinto is protean. There are sects and subsects, many esoteric. Streams of Shinto thought wind and twist, sometimes overlapping, sometimes crossed with imports like Taoism and Buddhism. Tracing a particular tributary back to a certain source is difficult, no less so because when it comes to a religion like Shinto, its springs hidden so far back in the past, the secret merges with the simply forgotten. Even in "mainstream" Shinto much is veiled. If you are not a *kannushi,* a priest, there is esotery to which you will never be privy, places within a shrine you will never go. And for only a very few Japanese are the details of Shinto worship and beliefs more than of passing concern. They go to shrines on special occasions, or to importune the deities there for some favor, or to give thanks for those received. But as an organized religion, Shinto does not play a formal role in the lives of most modern Japanese on a daily basis. One exception—and even that is becoming rare—is in the kamidana, the small shrine found in many Japanese homes and in other places, like the traditional dojo.

A word before we begin to think about the kamidana itself: the budoka must come to an accommodation with Shinto.

He need not, it is crucial to observe, embrace it as a religion. He may be a devout Christian or an unapologetic atheist or come from any manner of religious or spiritual background. He does not need to *believe* in the tenets or folklore or practices of Shinto. But he must have some familiarity with them because their influence in the dojo is pervasive. Consider it this way, if you are not an adherent to Shinto but wish to practice a budo: it is like living next to a big river, its banks right at the edge of your yard. You may not ever swim in the river or fish in it. Even so, you will be aware of it. You can tolerate it. Or enjoy it. Study it from the point of view of the observer or naturalist. Or take some kind of spiritual or emotional solace or satisfaction from its presence. Or regard it as just one more facet of your life with which you must deal. No matter how you consider it, however, that river is a part of your consciousness. You will be affected to some degree by it. (This should not be interpreted as a dire warning of impending apostasy for those with other religious convictions. The Baptist living in the United States, for example, may share precisely the same doctrines and faith as a Baptist in Africa. But it would be absurd to suppose his immersion in his own land's culture and his sense of being an American have no influence on his worship or his beliefs. They do not compromise or bastardize it. Surely, though, they inform it in ways that, while not specifically theological, make it unique.) So it is with the cultural and spiritual manifestations of Shinto in the dojo. The quiet simplicity of the dojo; the dictum that its environment, hot in the summer and cold in the winter is a reflection of the seasonal changes in nature; the sense that one's ancestors are to be kept in mind here in gratitude for the art they have passed down: all of these reflect values of Shinto thought. Yet while these are attitudes and behaviors in the dojo, usually the only concrete symbol of Shinto will be in the kamidana.

While Shinto as a religion has been a part of Japan since before history began there, as a focus of worship or reverence for one's ancestors, the kamidana does not have as long a history in Japan as might be supposed. Shinto, from its earliest development in prehistoric Japan, did not place much emphasis on individual centers or locales for the expression of religious concentration. The faithful went to a shrine near them for public rituals conducted by priests. The commemoration of a family's *sorei,* or ancestors, was largely confined to Buddhist rituals once that religion began to be assimilated in Japan in the sixth century. (Interestingly, the word *Shinto* does not seem to have had much if any use prior to this introduction of a foreign religion. Once Buddhism, or *Bukkyo-do*—the "Way of Buddha's Teachings," took hold, there was a need to discriminate in speaking of indigenous beliefs; hence *Shin-to* or the "Way of the Gods.") Prior to the eleventh century, most evidence indicates that when private homes had some need for a Shinto ceremony, a temporary shrine of some sort was erected within the home and kept there only for the course of the ritual itself. During the Heian era, however, the sect of Ise Shinto, which, along with the Izumo sect, are the two oldest forms of Shinto in Japan, began to stress the importance of having less centralized shrines as places of worship. This led to the promotion of including small shrines in homes. People started to reserve a shelf or *tana* (*-dana* is the suffix) for some kind of object that served as a focus for worshipping both their own familial ancestors and the local tutelary deities, both called, generically, *kami.*

Early forms of these kamidana looked more like cupboards and were called *todana.* In a few of the very oldest martial arts dojo devoted to the classical koryu still around in Japan, most of them on the private property of the lineal headmasters of the ryu, some todana are still in place. More commonly, however, households erected a shelf on the *kamoi,* the lintel beam of the house, for holding what amounted to a miniature version of a Shinto shrine. Inside the shrine were *kamifuda* or *gofu.* The former are paper talismans, the latter charms or amulets. Both were originally specific in nature, dedicated to the particular deities of a main Shinto shrine located nearby who were supposed to look over the affairs of the region or community. More commonly, the objects represented the kami that were familial ancestors, called *ujigami.*

One theory for the increasing popularity of household kamidana posits that they were a reaction by Shinto to the rise of Buddhism in Japan. Followers of the Buddha installed *butsudan,* or altars, in their homes. Butsudan were often elaborate, lacquered, and painted with gold leaf inside. They held the *ihai,* or ancestral tablets of a family. Perhaps fearing a loss of influence, Shinto priests may have encouraged the home installation of kamidana as a reminder of the faith that was close at hand. Unlike the butsudan, though, the kamidana, even in its earliest forms, was always made of plain wood or *shiraki*, a tradition that continues today. Kamidana are never painted or even stained. Thy are always natural in color. Kamidana were situated either in one of the main rooms of a home, facing the entrance, or near the kitchen since the hearth was spiritually at the center of the dwelling. They were installed either facing toward the front of the room as one entered (omote), or opposite, above the entrance, facing into the room (*kamite*). A dojo's kamidana will always be placed in the omote position, so one faces it upon entering the room. It should, however, be placed so it is facing south or east, and never north or west. (Why? It has to do with a Japanese sort of feng shui, a loose collection of strictures of geomancy that called, literally, for a place for everything and everything in its place. The location of a castle or house, the way a sumo ring is built and oriented, the placement of outbuildings around one's property: all these have specific rules. Some of these rules are native Japanese, consistent with folk beliefs; others are connected to Chinese Taoism. In a home or a structure like a dojo, south and east are propitious directions, just as north and west are thought to invite trouble.)

The kamidana is at the very center of the dojo in terms of that building's spiritual organization. It is placed far enough up on a wall to be safe from errant strikes from any weapons and also so that members are always before and below it. When entering or leaving a dojo, most forms of etiquette call for a bow in the direction of the kamidana, and class is always opened and closed with formal bows to it. And so what is it that is up there? Obviously, there is the shrine itself, the *kamidana-jinja*. There are several "styles." Most are based upon the basic forms of full-sized Shinto shrine architecture. The particular style to be found in the dojo will depend on either the personal preference of the teacher or on the affiliation or history of the art being practiced in that dojo. A general key to identification is in the roof or its features. Roofs with long, sloping fronts are *nagare-zukuri* style, probably the most common form of shrine in private homes. You may see shrines on the shelf with "horns" on either side of the roof (*shimmei* style) or with the horns on the front and back (*taisha* style), both very old examples of Shinto architecture. A broad roof with a small portico on the front is of the *Hachiman-zukuri* or Hachiman style. The second-century emperor, Ojin, his wife, and his mother comprise the center deities of this sect of Shinto. Since it has long been favored by the warrior and military class, some dojo kamidana are modeled in the Hachiman style. No matter what style, the kamidana will have doors on its front that are kept closed for all but special occasions. Inside are sometimes the kamifuda, or paper talismans, mentioned above, along with a round mirror, one of the three sacred regalia connected with the founding of Japan. The only other object actually inside the kamidana is a bit of cloth that is hung directly behind the doors, a *goshiki*, or "five brocade" banner, that acts as a final barrier between the outside world and the inner recesses of the shrine itself.

On either side of the shrine are—we're speaking typically here; not all kamidana shelves are arranged in exactly the same way, but we're using an ideal example—a pair of vases with short branches of leafy twigs in them. The vases are *sakaki tate;* the branches are from the *Cleyera japonica,* the sakaki tree. The sakaki is an evergreen. It is a member of the same family of plants as tea. In the mystical age of the gods of Japan that are recorded in the *Kojiki,* the goddess Amaterasu Omi-kami secreted herself in a cave over a dispute with her brother, plunging the world into darkness. To lure her out, the lesser deities hung mirrors from a tree and staged a dance, sending word to Amaterasu that there was a being even more beautiful than she performing outside her cave. Intrigued, Amaterasu ventured to the opening. She saw herself reflected in the mirrors and so she came out and light was restored. The tree holding the mirrors, according to the legend, was a sakaki. Further, because they are evergreen, sakaki figure in some Shinto rituals as reminders of life's continuity. (Though it might be churlish to observe it, sakaki branches on many kamidana shelves nowadays are even longer-lived since they are made of green plastic.)

Behind the sakaki vases are *heiji,* a pair of glass ewers with caps on them, both filled with *omiki,* or purified sake. Sake's association with Shinto is so fundamental it is impossible to imagine the latter without the former. Sake has always been credited as a gift from the kami. Sake was used to make drunk the eight-headed serpent that was terrorizing mythical Japan, enabling Susano to slay him. One explanation for the name of the drink itself is that *sa* was an early word to refer to the deity of rice plants while *ke* meant "food." Another is that *sake* came from *sakaeru,* a verb meaning "to prosper" or "to flourish," a reminder that where sake flowed, so too flowed the good life. As early as the Jomon period, farmers discovered that by chewing rice, then spitting it into a vessel, they could create the fermentation that made sake. While distinctly unappealing, this method was also understandably limited in making sake on any kind of large scale. So the saliva was later replaced with molds that activated the fermentation in a more sanitary and altogether palatable way. But given its purportedly sacred origins, sake made the good old-fashioned way continued to be used for ceremonial occasions. Rice chewed in the mouths of maidens was used for fermenting omiki, a libation for the gods. Japan is still a traditional place in many ways. But finding omiki manufactured through such personal attention would be an interesting discovery. Instead, omiki today is sake brewed the normal way but offered in a religious sense, as when it appears in the heiji bottles on the kamidana.

A flat dish in front of the center of the shrine contains raw rice, or *kome.* Just as with sake, rice's association with life in Japan is well known; it is natural for it to be placed on the kamidana as a symbol and as something of an offering. On the front and to the left is a *mizutama,* a roundish glass bottle with a pointed cap that is a little more than half filled with water. On the other side is another plate, heaped with salt. Both water and salt are used in Shinto's purification rites. Sumotori, for example, rinse their mouths with water before a bout to cleanse themselves of any evil intentions, and they scatter salt in the ring to clear it of malevolent spirits.

These instruments in front of and around the kamidana-jinja are collectively known as *shinki*. Along with them you might see *ofuda*, or "wooden tablets," inscribed with the name of a deity or a Shinto shrine, which are thought to represent the "essence" of the kami. Candles or small lamps, often in the form of the real ones seen at the entrance of Shinto shrines, are also sometimes found at the kamidana, just for show or, connected to an electrical outlet, as a source of light for special ceremonies. *Ozen* are short-legged trays that are placed on or near the kamidana for *osonaemono*, or offerings, though unless the teacher or owner of the dojo is a rather devout practitioner of Shinto, few martial arts training halls will follow this custom. Just in case, though, if there are offerings made of fresh foods, it is usually cooked rice, which should be placed in a bowl on the tray in the mornings (and eaten later on). Salt is replaced on the first of each month. Any foods from the ocean or the mountains are replaced in the middle of the month. The only other special attention given a kamidana is when it is wrapped in white paper for a certain length of time, a ritual known as *kamidana-fuji*. This is done at the death of either the dojo's teacher or a senior member. The ritual has its roots in Shinto's aversion to death as a source of impurity. The paper is meant to protect the shrine in these circumstances.

The kamidana is not really complete without a section of woven rice straw hung either below the shelf or on wooden posts above it and called a *shimenawa*. To return to an example we have used before, if you look at the impressive waists of the top ranks of sumotori, you will notice a thick rope wrapped around them. These are *yokozuna*, or "sideways ropes," and are exclusively the property of the champions, who take their title of yokozuna after the woven strands of rope. The derivation of the shimenawa comes from the same story mentioned above, that of the Shinto goddess Amaterasu, sulking in her cave over a fight with her obstreperous brother. Amaterasu was lured out of the cave by the mirrors and the dancing: when she appeared, the other deities immediately threw a rope across the entrance so she could not return. The shimenawa, then, represents a boundary, a border. (Actually, the word is written with characters, the second of which is "rope," the first of which means "flowing," an intriguing choice that reinforces the fluidity of Shinto's doctrines.) In Shinto terms, a shimenawa delineates a special place. It designates an area set aside. For demonstrations of classical arts at a tutelary shrine, the demonstration area is often marked by a thin shimenawa wrapped around four bamboo poles to make a rectangle. Since, if you are in a traditional dojo and training there regularly, you will spend a lot of time sitting or standing facing in the direction of the kamidana, you will have plentiful opportunities to examine the shimenawa there. First, notice that if it is of a style where the lay of the rope goes from thicker to thin, the thick end will usually be placed to your right. Second, notice that the lay of the rope itself is typically to the left. There are varying theories as to the origin of these conventions. The thicker end of the same shimenawa will, of course, be on the left side of the shrine from the perspective of the shrine itself, with the rope strands twisting to the right. There is considerable symbolism, some of it secret within the lore of Shinto and known only to priests, about the relationship between left and right, and this may be an example.

You will also notice that decorating the shimenawa are zigzagging strips of twisted or folded white paper. These are *gohei* or *shide*. There isn't a clear explanation for their origin. The prevalent theory is that they represent streaks of lightning, a sign of fertility. The same yokozuna rope wrapped around the waist of the champion sumotori is decorated with these gohei as well. The shimenawa and its hanging paper gohei, in fact, are seen all over Japan in places deemed of particular spiritual importance. Grand shrines have them hung on the lintels or arches, the ropes as big around as a ship's hawser. They can be found wrapped around trees or boulders as well, when those objects are believed to contain the spirits of deities and are deserving of commemoration. In the dojo the shimenawa at the front of the kamidana set aside that area of space and give it the air of importance it should have. Note, however, that on those occasions when by some circumstance the kamidana is hit by a weapon or otherwise accidentally knocked over, there is no need for the guilty party to commit suicide on the spot or perform any groveling act of contrition. Shinto is, as we've noted, a celebration of the natural cycles of life. And things falling and breaking is part of that process. When it happens, the implements are simply returned to their place, or replaced if they have broken, and life goes on. Likewise, while one ought to be careful and sober around the kamidana, it is not an "off-limits" area per se, even though the teacher or senior students may be the ones who take care of it, cleaning and dusting and attending to it. Understandably, the visitor to the dojo will not go over to look at the kamidana like it was a museum piece: it has a deep meaning for the members there and their feelings should be respected. And if you are invited to look at it, it should not be touched.

There is a correct way to bow to the kamidana, a process that at first might seem complicated and intricate but which will quickly become a habit. It's *nirei* ("two bows"), *nihyakushu* ("two claps"), and *ichirei* ("one bow"). Bow twice, either standing or sitting, then clap twice, then bow a final time. This is the same way one bows at an outdoor Shinto shrine. The first two bows are meant as a way of announcing yourself, the claps are to bring the attention of the spirits within, and the final bow is a polite way of closing. Most training sessions are begun and conclude with this ritual. The clapping itself is called *kashiwade*. The whole procedure of bowing to the shrine is a form of etiquette known in Japanese as *hairei*.

You should not be surprised or disappointed if your dojo does not have the kamidana we've described here. You should be surprised and disappointed if you go into a dojo that has at its front wall trinkets or doodads; or posters; or statuary of Buddha or Hotei; or gaudy, ersatz friezes of dragons, cobras, tigers, and all manner of bestiary. Such efforts to make a kamidana wall more "Oriental" may be sincere. But they are profoundly inappropriate and, almost without exception, shockingly tacky. To be sure, not all dojo in Japan have kamidana and in fact public dojo are by law prohibited from displaying any kind of Shinto shrine. This was a mandate of the Occupation forces who knew too well the unhealthy relationship between state-sponsored Shinto and Japan's militarism of the last century. Public and school dojo in Japan have a Japanese flag on the wall where a kamidana might be, or even nothing at all. In the United States, some dojo may eschew a traditional kamidana for religious reasons or because they do not know how to set one up. Instead of a kamidana, other dojo might have a portrait of the founder of their art or a scroll of calligraphy. While these objects may lack the spiritual significance of a proper kamidana, they nevertheless represent an attempt to designate a part of the dojo as a place set aside. The area becomes a dimension of the space that is given to matters that, while they may not be immediately practical or obvious in the dojo, are fundamental to budo.

The serious budoka's attitude toward the kamidana may best be summarized by the Japanese word *iyamau*. In our age, the character for this word is pronounced *uyamau*. But the derivation is informative. Originally, the word meant to convey or express respect through one's behavior or posture or carriage. Now, *uyamau* has come to refer more to the actual feeling of respect itself. In the evolution of the word, the outward manifestation has resolved into the actual expression itself. The beginner in the dojo is apt to approach hairei, the ceremonial bowing to the kamidana, and the kamidana itself as an incidental part of training. It is a ritual. Vaguely "religious," though he isn't sure how. There may be a frisson of the exotic about it at the start, or some doubt about the appropriateness of the task in light of one's own religious or spiritual inclinations. Still, if one is determined to follow the Way, he goes about the task of bowing and clapping, cleaning the shelf if that chore is assigned to him. Again and again he goes through the motions and, as he learns more about the art, its origination and lore, about those who have gone before him, his thoughts turn from time to time to the meaning behind the symbolism. What was once an odd practice— bowing in the direction of the kamidana—slowly becomes imbued with a deeper significance. Not every time. There are training sessions when he is in a hurry to get on with the actual practice and others when he is hasty to get the ceremonial folderol over with so he can go home. It will always be like that. And he must have a natural inclination toward thinking or looking more deeply and, if he does not, the concept behind the kamidana might always be hidden or disregarded. Chances are, though, that if he sticks around the budo long enough, his character will lead him to a more intense evaluation of everything that goes on in the dojo, including the rituals before the kamidana. Gradually, as the formalities there become a part of his normal behavior in the dojo, he senses something. And probably without his being entirely aware of it, the consciousness of it all becomes evident—in his posture, in his attitudes, in his interactions with those around him. Through the aegis of outer form comes an inner transformation. While his religious beliefs may be entirely divorced from the doctrines of Shinto, sitting and bowing before the kamidana he is nonetheless changed. He is brought into the stream, the flow of life that is represented in the symbol of the kamidana.

7

CONTEMPLATION

MOKUSO

MOKUSOOO!!!

In many dojo, this word is roared like a battle cry. It comes twice, at the beginning of a practice session and again at the end, always after students in the dojo have lined up and are quietly sitting. To get them into that position, other commands are sometimes given. *"Yame"* or *"Keiko osame"* is shouted to signal that the session is over. *Narande* means "line up." *Seiretsu* or *keiretsu* are commands to line up according to rank. *Chakuza* means to kneel down and take the sitting position of *seiza*. Once seated, there is a long moment of settling in as the rustling and groans of exertion and labored breathing fade, followed by a silence that is broken by the shout that seems to penetrate right into the bodies of those seated.

MOKUSOOO!!!

The *moku* of *mokuso* means "to silence." *So* means "thoughts." *Mokuso* is sometimes thought of as a period of "meditation." In a way, it is. A better way to think of it might be to consider it as a transitional period. Many believe the dojo is a place of refuge, a place where the concerns of every-day life can be put aside. This can lead to some incorrect as-sumptions, though. The dojo is not an escape from everyday life. Rather it is a place where one can *confront* the realities of our daily living, meet them in concentrated form, and learn to deal with them. The dojo is a microcosm, intensified, of our day-to-day existence and activities. As such, we approach what goes on there with more focus and intensity than we might other areas of our lives. That requires a period of tran-sition and that is what the moments of mokuso are all about. When we begin, the period of mokuso allows us to silence whatever aggravations, concerns, desires, or anticipations we have had outside the dojo, to put them aside for the course of our practice. When we finish that practice, another period of mokuso allows us to reemerge, to come back to our lives outside the dojo. There is nothing particularly "mystical" or even transcendent in mokuso. We are not striving for enlight-enment in our sitting as might the Zen acolyte. We are merely transitioning, moving from one place into another: neither special, neither extraordinary, but both are funda-mental parts of our day.

What do we think about while sitting in mokuso? If you ask, the teacher might say, "Think about nothing." Easier said than done. Thoughts come crowding in, pushing their way to vie for our attention. We wonder, beginning class in mokuso, if we should not have skipped training altogether this evening. A report at work or school is due; the laundry's been neglected all week. When we finish and are once again sitting, we're concerned with how well we did. Was the sensei satisfied? Are we improving? It is extremely difficult not to entertain such thoughts. Trying not to have them seems to make them spring up all the more ferociously. Under such circumstances, we might want to consider a concept that comes from chado, the Way of tea. "Ichi-go; ichi-e" means "one encounter; one chance." During your day outside the dojo, you had one opportunity to approach the tasks that needed tending. One opportunity to interact with others. In the dojo, it is the same. This practice session came only once in your life. Next time, even if it is the next evening, you will be different; the lesson will be different. It will be the same, of course, in your life outside the dojo. Each moment is unique. In mokuso, we have a moment to consider: did we make the most of each moment before we came to the dojo? Once there and once finished with our practice, we can reflect again. Did we use each moment of the class to our best? If so, we can be content. If not, the next class, the next day, will present us with the opportunity to try it again. We may never be able to achieve the "no-mind" state of quietude of the Zen master in our mokuso. But if we use the periods of mokuso to accept the transitory nature of our world and to embrace it, then they will never be moments that have been wasted.

8

BOWING

OJIREI

In 1908, a New England schoolmarm, Alice Bacon, was asked to come to teach at the Tokyo Peeress's Academy. In a letter home, she described the rituals of the bow at this elite girls' school:

> "When the bell rings I go to my recitation room and there, ranged in line outside the door, is my class awaiting me. I bow as low as I can. The pupils bow still lower, then go into the room. They take their places quietly and stand; I bow from my place at the teacher's desk, again the girls bow, and take their seats. When I finish the lesson I bow to the class, who all bow in reply, rise and march quietly out the door to arrange themselves in order and wait for me. I walk out, bow to them once more, and they make a farewell obeisance as well. The whole thing is very pretty and I am charmed with this manner of calling to order and dismissing classes. It might have a civilizing effect if introduced to American schools."

Despite Ms. Bacon's suggestion, bowing did not become a part of the American educational process. Indeed, except for circumstances that are about as rare as the doffing of top hats, bowing has never really been a part of Western etiquette. We tend to associate it with either extravagant, theatrical gestures, like the cavalier grandly bowing to "My Lady," or with the ham actor taking his exaggerated bow at the end of his performance. To see a Western male bowing today is only slightly less rare than seeing a woman making the female version of the gesture, the curtsy. Consequently, most Westerners are at a disadvantage in bowing. In Japan, toddlers are bent into the appropriate posture by parents until the movement becomes almost instinctual. Ethnologists note the habit may even begin earlier, since traditionally babies were carried *onbu*-style, on their mother's back, and so they would have been bowing, in a sense, each time their mother did. Even so, with the exception of those involved in traditional arts like the tea ceremony, or martial arts, the average Japanese of our present generation isn't all that skilled in this fine art, either. Parents complain that the younger generation hasn't the polish in performing the *ojirei*, or bow, that was once standard everywhere in Japan, performed dozens of times during the course of a day. Department store elevator girls must train with special hinged gauges to teach them the exact angle of a bow so they can correctly greet customers entering the elevators. In most cases they no longer learn the proper way to do it at home. Certainly few Japanese today could pass muster among their ancestors from the feudal period.

Bowing, as a form of obeisance and later of greeting, can be found in numerous cultures. It is ubiquitous in much of

Asia. The bow was formalized initially during the Muro-machi age, the long period of Japan's history that saw the rise of the military class and its rule by a succession of shogun of the Ashikaga family, which governed the land from 1338 until 1573. Ogasawara Sadamune (1294–1350) was an ally of the first Ashikaga shogun, Takauji. Sadamune was instrumental in elevating a cousin of the shogun's, Kougon, to the imperial throne. In gratitude for his services, and probably because he recognized the talents of Sadamune, the shogun appointed Sadamune as the official in charge of matters of etiquette within the ranks of the shogun's retainers. The great-grand-son of Sadamune, Ogasawara Nagahide (1366–1424) contin-ued in this office and wrote the first comprehensive text on etiquette, the *Sangi Itto,* around 1380. We may find all this more than a little stuffy and silly and effeminate, picturing a prissy, slightly fey Nagahide sitting around and fussing over whether this particular form of bow was appropriate at that time or whether it ought to be something else. Notions of such priggery, though, should be leavened if we know what is meant by the title of Nagahide's work. *Sangi Itto* means "Three Arts as One." The three arts were etiquette (and eth-ics, considered an aspect of the former), horsemanship, and archery. As famous as the Ogasawara family was for their knowledge of etiquette and manners, they were samurai. The Ogasawara were widely respected as fighters, and regarded for their ability to wield a bow and to ride a horse into battle in such a way that the animal became a weapon as much as it was a means of transportation. The Ogasawara were warriors.

Their etiquette was not an affectation. It was a means by which the samurai could be safe around other fighting men and could, simultaneously, signal a lack of malicious intent on his part among others as well, if he wished to do so. Significantly, it was a tradition of the Ogasawara family and the ryu they founded that all three arts were to be mastered fully and represented by a single inheritor who was responsible for the ryu named after them. No doubt fearing that etiquette without martial skill was nothing but pomposity—while its opposite would have been barbarism—the Ogasawara were careful to transmit all of their arts in equal measure and to have at their head a man who was competent in all. (In the 1960s, a descendant of Sadamune laid claim to the headmastery of only one third of the Ogasawara ryu, that part dealing with etiquette. It was a startling development in the history of the ryu, one with wide repercussions in the world of traditional Japan. While the matter was never conclusively resolved, most of those concerned with such things have continued to accept the headmaster of the ryu as the man who has inherited all facets of it.)

For centuries, the conventions of Ogasawara ryu manners were taught only to the nobility and to the samurai class in Japan. It wasn't until the Edo period, when the merchant class had amassed enough wealth to afford to study etiquette as a discrete activity, that the ryu finally began instructing those not of the warrior caste. Unfortunately, this opening of the Ogasawara ryu to commoners had a deleterious effect on the ryu and on the whole concept of formal manners in

Japan. Prior to that time, the varied conventions of bowing, a central part of the samurai's etiquette, were seen as a masculine, even kind of *macho* quality. They were, after all, the property of the elite samurai who, for better or worse, were perceived as something special. Once they were introduced to the general public, the etiquette of the ryu soon came to be viewed as an affectation of the leisure classes. As Western ideas of egalitarianism and individuality were introduced to Japan, the conventions of formal etiquette fell even further from favor with the masses. Much as mannered social customs in the West came in for some disdain during the sixties in Europe and America, and even as a subtle form of class oppression, traditional etiquette in a Japan once introduced to Western ideas was treated with some contempt.

Even those of a conservative bent and who have the sensibilities of Miss Manners would find all the intricacies of the Ogasawara ryu to be a bit much. There are, for example, nine separate ways of bowing from a seated position, according to the ryu's teachings. For those who use them daily, like advanced practitioners of the tea ceremony, they appear natural and graceful. For most of us, they are awkward and stilted. The dicta regarding their use are not particularly of benefit for the average guy. (Know, too, that the very mention of "Ogasawara ryu" carries a pejorative connotation to some Japanese. They associate it with a rigid protocol and stilted, feudalistic manners that have little place, aside from class snobbery, in the modern world.) Fortunately, in the dojo the conventions of bowing, while based almost entirely on the models of the Ogasawara ryu, are comparatively simple. That is not to say, though, that they are easy. Basic instruction can and must be given in the dojo. The beginner must remember a number of points until they become unconscious habit. When making a standing bow, or *ritsu-rei*, sometimes called a *ryurei*, or a seated one, called *za-rei*, keep this advice in mind: *Don't keep your hands stiffly at your sides, or let them dangle.* If you are standing, allow them to slide, palms down along the sides of your thighs. If you are seated, the hands go from your thighs down to the ground in front of you. Too often, Japanese martial arts incorrectly or inadequately taught adopt a pseudo-military pose, or some other affectations. One of these is the silly habit of slapping the sides of one's thighs upon bowing. Since the meaning of the bow is as a demonstration of humility, this "look at me!" gesture is particularly ludicrous.

Don't bob spastically. Lower your torso as smoothly as fitness, girth, and the condition of your spine will permit. Pause, then straighten at the same speed. The back of your neck should be roughly on the same plane as your spine when you bow. In other words, don't nod or dip your head. The incline of you entire upper torso and your head should be the same. Some newcomers to the world of the budo may be told that in bowing, a martial artist needs never to take his eyes off his opponent since this can result in an unexpected attack. Unfortunately, many teachers who may not have had very good instruction repeat this information and so there are training halls filled with people bowing to one another in an awkward way, craning their necks to keep in sight their training partners. Bowing to one another should take place with proper distancing. You should be far enough away from the other person so you can bow correctly and still keep them in your peripheral vision. When standing, a good way to learn this distancing is to come only close enough to the person so that you can see his feet if you are both standing. From that distance, you should be able to bow and keep him fully in your sight peripherally.

Bow more fully to those who are senior to you in the dojo. If they are very senior, as in the case of a visiting teacher or some other dignitary within the art, you will bow lower than you would to your seniors or your regular teacher. But in most instances, a bow to a senior is made more appropriate not by bending lower but rather by holding the position of the bow at its lowest point a little longer than the person to whom you are bowing.

Even with this basic information and instruction, however, the details of making a correct ojirei can only be learned by osmosis. One must watch others who know how to do it and copy them. Some dojo will use a version of an Ogasawara-style seated bow that was used in certain situations where the person to whom one is bowing might have hostile intentions. From a sitting position on the floor with the lower legs bent fully under the thighs—it is called *seiza* and we'll go more deeply into it in a moment—and hands on the thighs, the left hand moves down to the floor first, then the right, then comes a bow with one's forehead placed approximately over a triangle formed by the thumbs and forefingers of both hands spread out. Coming up from the bow the order is reversed; the right hand moves back to the thigh, then the left. The rationale for the sequence is putatively martial. Performing the bow in such a way, assuming one is wearing a sword thrust through the sash on the left side of the body, keeps the right hand and arm free and unencumbered as much as possible. (For the same reason, the etiquette of this particular bow requires the person to kneel down, first on the left knee, then the right, when taking a seated position, and to reverse that coming up.) Keeping the hands flat on the floor but close enough so one's head is over them while prostrating ensures they can be brought into use quickly. It all may seem paranoid at our remove. But during Japan's long, long period of internecine warfare, treachery was literally a way of life. Even the smallest opening in posture or comportment was dangerous. Notice, however, that I said this was a "putative" explanation. There are other theories for the evolution of this bow. Given the martial circumstances under which the Ogasawara ryu developed, ours is a reasonable conclusion. But in any event, do not use the bow as some kind of aggressive display. And don't enter into it with the hair-trigger mentality that deadly ninja may be waiting to spring into action to try to assassinate you as you bow. Note, too, that some dojo eschew the alternate left-right placement of the hands when bowing to the dojo shrine or to a teacher or even to one another in daily training since none of these are "enemies" even in a potential way.

At the opening and closing of training sessions, bows are announced by oral commands in some dojo. You might hear "shinzen ni rei" (bow to the kamidana or front of the dojo), "sensei ni rei" (bow to the teacher), or "otagai ni rei" (bow to one another). Other times, the dojo member is expected to know when to bow without any command, such as when entering or leaving the training area or to a partner before and after the practice. Some dojo expect members to bow to one another even outside the dojo, or to bow to the sensei no matter where you might see him. Others find this affected, and probably most mature budoka would agree.

While the influences of the Ogasawara ryu were pervasive within the world of the samurai, the dictates of that ryu were by no means followed by all of the warrior caste in Japan. Many classical martial ryu developed outside the big-city sphere of influence of the Ogasawara way of doing things. Their bowing etiquette copied local custom. (Ryu that originated in rural areas can sometimes be distinguished by their bows. Because they trained outside, where sitting formally on muddy, rough ground would have been impractical, these ryu might opt for a bow from a squatting position.) Some ryu used a variation of sumo's elaborate *chirichozu* bowing ritual that still begins all bouts of that art. Squatting on the balls of the feet, the practitioners bow by touching the hands to the ground or keeping them on the knees. Aficionados of historical dramas from Japan will also recognize some methods of bowing that were used by men in armor, like kneeling on one knee and touching a single hand to the ground. If weapons are involved in the bowing ritual, placing them on the ground beside or in front of oneself or holding them will also have an influence on the way the bow is performed. *Gaku-rei* or *nuka-rei* is a full prostration in which the seated bow is so deep the forearms touch the ground along with the hands. (*Gaku* and *nuka* here both refer to the forehead, since the bow goes so deep that it comes into contact with or at least close to the floor.) Probably the only place this bow is seen in modern budo is in the sword-drawing art of iaido, where it is sometimes used as a ritualistic bow to one's sword, has been placed out on the floor in front of the practitioner. Unless there is a clear historical link within the art, there is little need to artificially adopt any of these alternative methods, however, just for the sake of "looking martial."

The majority of budo dojo will, in one way or another, use some form of bowing, mentioned above, that will require you to sit on your lower legs in the position of seiza. The characters used to write it are informative. The first means "proper"; the latter means "seated posture." Not coincidentally, the word can be written with a different first character that means "quiet." So it's "proper sitting," or "quiet sitting." Its etymology aside, seiza can be hell. Alessandro Valignano (1539–1606), a Jesuit administrator who spent years in late sixteenth-century Japan spreading the faith, described it this way: "Their way of sitting causes no less suffering because they kneel on the floor and sit back on their heels. This is a very restful position for them but for others it is very wearisome and painful." It is very likely you will be among those "others." There is nothing to be done about it, however, but to get started and to learn how to do it.

Seiza actually begins with kneeling. As we described above, from a standing position, the left knee drops first, according to the Ogasawara tradition. In other forms of etiquette, including those preferred by most schools of the tea ceremony, one kneels almost at the same time onto both knees, with the left touching the ground just ahead of the right. In some traditions, this kneeling starts with you standing, both heels touching. In others, you move one foot back just slightly before you kneel—the foot moving being the one farthest away from either whatever senior person is in the room or, depending on where you are in the room, relative to the kamidana. Why not kneel by taking a big step forward or back and then going down on one knee so it is right beside the other foot, which would be a more comfortable way of getting down? Try this with a kimono on and you will see that it is difficult to do without creating a big gap in the lower lapels of the kimono, allowing anyone in front of you a possibly unwelcome view.

As the right knee touches, you squat back, resting your buttocks on your heels. Your toes at this point are all folded away from your foot and not lying flat on the floor. This posture is called *kiza*. Kiza is the position, in the days of the samurai, in which the warrior most often kept himself when sitting formally. For seiza, it is an intermediary step. After you are in kiza, your toes are straightened back again, and once they are flat on the floor, you settle back on them, sitting so both heels are squarely below each buttock, feet folded over so the big toes of one cross over those of the other.

You have to practice this until each step flows into the next. It is not easy to do. In the Ogasawara tradition, a sheet of paper is sometimes laid down just ahead of where your knees touch the floor and you are required to kneel so smoothly and quietly that the paper doesn't move from any air you might stir up. Once you are seated, your posture will need some adjusting. Do not slump. Do not sit so erect your belly presses forward. Don't stick your chin out. The best, though not necessarily most pleasant, way to assume the correct posture is to imagine there is an eyelet in the very top of your skull connected to a rope that is stretching you up to the ceiling. Or imagine the floor and ceiling are pressing gently together and it is only your posture holding them apart, your spine stretched, though not beyond its natural curve. Tuck in your chin. Imagine you are wearing loose earrings and that if they fall, they will drop from your lobes into the space right behind your clavicle. Hands belong on your thighs. Oftentimes young, tough karateka will pose in seiza with their fists resting on their thighs. Don't emulate them, even if you are a young, tough karateka. Keep both arms at your sides, with just enough pressure to imagine you are cradling eggs against your armpits: hold them tight enough to keep from falling, not so tight the shells are crushed. The knees are placed just far enough apart so you would have enough room to place your fists, side by side, between them if you are a male; closer if you are a female. (Again, this is a prescription of the Ogasawara method. Some dojo may not make a gender distinction. But know that a woman sitting with her knees apart does not look "proper" in the context of most traditional Japanese arts, while a man sitting with his pressed together would look equally odd.) Drop your shoulders. Drop them some more. Most modern people, especially Westerners, tend to develop postures standing or sitting in which the shoulders are high. Particularly when we are trying to be "formal." Consciously try to take any stiffness out of your shoulders and let them come down from your spine. As you do this, you will find your spine tends to straighten, as it should.

We have already described the ojirei, the actual bow, from the position of seiza. Perhaps the commonest errors are breaking the line of the back of the head and the back as you bow and raising your buttocks off your heels at the same time. In between times, when you are simply sitting—many dojo will have you in seiza for a moment of meditation before and after training, and there is a chapter here on that—you will quickly learn about the challenge of seiza. It is so familiar there is a word in Japanese specifically to describe the sensation of your legs going to sleep in this position: *shibireru*. Before they go off on the nod, however, there are the aches, cramps, throbs, annoying pains in ankles and knees, and you'll hear from muscles in your lower half that haven't gotten your attention in years, if ever. It is not unbearable. But, depending upon your flexibility, weight, and general fitness level, it *is* uncomfortable. Most Japanese today cannot sit comfortably in seiza. It is not a posture we take in daily life. So it requires some getting used to. There is no shortcut, no secret. Concentrate on the alignment of your head and shoulders and limit yourself at first to a few minutes in the position. Try it on carpet or a rug at first. Over time, seiza will become more natural for you. It may never be a position in which you want to sit down and watch a movie. But in most instances, your body will eventually learn seiza.

Once you have bowed, you must get up again. If you are unaccustomed to getting to your feet from seiza, you will come up so you're kneeling on one knee, the other leg bent out in front of you so you can push off and up to standing. This would be easy. But of course, it isn't the Ogasawara way. Actually, it is not a very effective way to stand from a martial point of view as well as from an aesthetic one, since it is easy to see the leg on which the majority of your balance rests for a moment. Your posture will have placed you in a position where you can be tripped or knocked over. Instead, rise back up to kiza. Then shuffle your right leg forward so the ball of your right foot rests on the ground, toes bent, at a level right next to the bottom of your left calf. From here, you rise *straight* up. Try it facing a wall about a foot or so in front of you. If you are standing correctly—"like a column of smoke rising" according to the Ogasawara ryu—you should not bump the wall with your knee or anything else. To be able to sink into and rise out of seiza gracefully and with balance is a skill no less demanding than sitting in the position and bowing properly. You should practice it when the opportunity presents itself, not just at the beginning and end of class. You may never measure up to the demands of the Ogasawara of old. But you will be doing a great deal to make your body more supple and disciplined and amenable to the demands of budo.

Beginners and even those with a great deal of experience both need to be careful about the overuse of a bow as well as its misuse. In some dojo, if training is going on and a teacher comes by to make a correction or give instruction, the student bows. In some dojo, any students standing nearby who hear the comments of the teacher bow as well. In some dojo, students are bowing and bobbing in what looks like something of a caricature. While all this bowing might be a sign of genuine respect, it can easily become an affectation. More importantly, when one is constantly bowing to a teacher or a senior, it works to create an attitude in the dojo that is not entirely healthy or in keeping with the spirit of budo. All those in the dojo should be mindful that the *ukerei* ("receiving bow") and the *okuri-rei* ("bestowed bow") are two wheels on the same axle. The student is properly grateful for the instruction; the teacher must be equally grateful at having those around him who are dedicated to the continuance of the art. Bowing continually to a teacher in situations when he does not return the courtesy can soon lead to the sense that the teacher "deserves" an obeisance. It can destroy the affinity between a teacher and his or her students. Those in a modern dojo should always bear in mind that the origination of all of Japan's martial Ways, as we've already noted, came from small, deeply integrated family and community units, mutually dependent upon one another. Hierarchical structure is vital in the dojo. Yet if it is enforced through a contrived etiquette that serves to remind students of their obligation while ignoring the concomitant obligations of the teacher, the results are bound to be quite inconsistent with the values of the budo.

Some newcomers to the dojo might object to bowing because they perceive in it a religious significance. Others might be left cold at the thought that in bowing to a teacher or a senior they are performing some sort of obeisance that is unseemly in a democratic society. Still others might wonder why we bow to one another in the dojo before and after training when a handshake might be more culturally appropriate. The responses to these objections are conclusive, though they may not be persuasive to the beginner. The "religious" significance to the ojirei is similar to that of maintaining a quiet composure in a church or other place of worship. By demonstrating respect in your posture and conduct you are not necessarily complicit in actually worshipping there: it's just the way you behave. The fact that believers might bow at a Shinto shrine or in a Buddhist temple in Japan does not mean that bowing is, in itself, a religious act. It is not. It is a way of greeting or acknowledgment and has been for many, many centuries. Is it democratic in the sense that you must prostrate yourself before someone else? No. The budo are not democratic. Their roots are in feudalism. No matter how modern they have become and how much they may continue to evolve, if they lose contact with those roots—and bowing is one way of maintaining that contact—they will no longer be budo. And that is why, as well, a handshake is not an appropriate substitute for a bow in the dojo. The act of bowing conveys feelings and attitudes that cannot be demonstrated with a handshake or some other form of greeting. The bow is unique. Learn to do it correctly. And heed the example of Araki Murashige, who found in the formal ritual of the bow a method with eventual implications somewhat beyond simple etiquette.

Late in the sixteenth century, the short-tempered shogun Oda Nobunaga had all of Japan in an uproar. One of his samurai, Araki Murashige, was in a particularly tight spot. That wasn't surprising: Araki had his hand in more than a dozen schemes and political intrigues at the time. One or more had come to the attention of his lord, Nobunaga, who called the samurai before him. For any of these men, including Araki, that meant checking his sword at the door before coming into the presence of Nobunaga. Unarmed, he kneeled to bow at the entrance of Nobunaga's chambers. It was a perilous moment, though there was no way for Araki to have known that other than—we must guess—through a finely developed sense of recognizing the possible presence of danger. Nobunaga was a master of the surprise attack. In fact, he had a couple of men standing at either side of the thick, wooden-paneled doors that slid together to be closed. Araki was required to bow from a seated position before entering, putting his head, literally, on the line of the threshold. Nobunaga's plan was to have both men slam the sliding doors together at just that moment, snapping Araki's neck.

Araki, whatever his failings, was not stupid. As I said, his antennae must have been out and sensitized for potential threats. And fortunately for his sake, he was well trained in the etiquette of the day. Following correct form, before bowing he pulled from his belt a folded fan men usually carried with them at that time, and carefully situated it in front of him.

Crack!

Both doors slammed shut—almost. Araki's fan was wedged right into the track of the doors, holding them just far enough apart to save his neck.

According to the story, the denouement of the incident had Araki maintaining his cool, rising up from the bow as if nothing at all had happened. He pulled it off so neatly that Nobunaga forgave him on the spot and appointed him to a government post. We are more than four centuries since Araki used the etiquette of a bow to escape. Few lives are on the line now. Even so, the implications of a bow properly done have far greater significance than as a greeting or acknowledgment. Learning to do it correctly is an essential step in following the Way.

9

MARTIAL LANGUAGE

HEIGO

H*eigo* means "martial language," or "military language." It is one of many such "languages" within Japanese. More accurately, heigo is a form of *ben,* a specialized dialect or lingua franca. There is, for example, *sushi-ben,* the slang used in sushi circles, where *shoyu* (soy sauce) is called *murasaki* (literally "purple") and instead of counting *ichi, ni, san,* it's *pin, ichinoji, geta.* These specialized slang forms evolved over years in Japan. Some are ancient, like the particular dialect used within the imperial household. Others, like the idioms used by young people, are so fresh and inventive they have already mutated and grown by the time anyone thinks to remark about them. In part, these "inside" ways of speaking have to do with the strong sense of belonging to a group that has long characterized Japanese civilization. Within the military and, to a lesser extent, the world of some colleges and universities with strong martial arts traditions, heigo is often used.

Heigo includes specific military terms like the Japanese equivalents for *corporal* or *battalion.* In some instances, though, heigo is almost indistinguishable from the rough, masculine Japanese used by young men. Instead of saying *"Yoroshii"* ("That's good" or "You're doing it right") as one might in gentler circumstances, the teacher in the dojo might grunt *"Yosh!"* In other instances, heigo uses different words entirely than in normal Japanese speech. *Zenpo* and *koho,* for example, are used instead of the Japanese equivalents for "forward" and "to the rear." They might be recognized by the average Japanese, but they would be used typically only in military circles or in the dojo. Just as the Japanese burglar's reference to lockpicks by the underworld slang term *shippiki* to demonstrate his "in" status in that criminal community, the budoka's familiarity with heigo used in the dojo is a way of identifying himself as an insider. However, there are two very important considerations he must bear in mind. First, the budoka must understand that these words are apt to be utterly incomprehensible to a native Japanese speaker without experience in the budo. They are not a part of normal vocabulary and you must not expect Japanese to know what you're talking about if you use them. Secondly, you ought to be aware of the context in which the word is used.

Which brings us to the matter of *Osu!* A staggering volume of words have been written supposedly to explain this interjection. In some dojo, particularly in karate dojo, it is used endlessly and ubiquitously, to mean everything from "I understand" to "I'll try" to "Hello" to "Goodbye" to "Yes, Sir!" to, presumably, "My foot aches." In others, it is used

primarily as a greeting, if at all. In some dojo, you will hear
people shouting "Osu!" hundreds of times in a single class;
in others, if someone uses it at all they are met with a laugh
or a snarl and a warning not to "talk that way here."

In all probability, *osu* began as a greeting. It is most likely
a contraction of *Ohayo gozaimasu,* or "Good morning." We
know it was used this way at Japan's prestigious naval academy going back to the early part of the twentieth century at
least. It may also be a compacted version of *O-negai shimasu,*
used in the dojo as a way of requesting a partner to train with
you. It is true that the kanji pronounced "osu" in combination can be written to mean "to push" and "to persevere."
To infer anything from that in an etymological sense, though,
is pure speculation with no evidence to support it. Think of it
this way: In English, we greet one another with, among other
salutations, "Good morning." Frequently we abbreviate this
to "Morning." Suppose I was a nonnative speaker, one with
a good command of English vocabulary and a desire to teach
it in my country, but with limited experience in its context.
I heard the greeting "Morning," during a time I was around
Americans and added it to my vocabulary. When I returned
to my native country and began to teach others to speak English, I informed my classes that "Morning" was a proper
way to greet a person. I knew this because I had heard it so
used. I didn't understand that "Morning" was not a universally correct greeting, however. It isn't used at night or, for
example, by a private speaking to a captain in the army. My
students would not understand this, either. Further, as they

began to teach English on their own, they would incorporate "Morning" into their lessons. Sooner or later, one of their students would say, "Why do they say that in English? What does a time of day have to do with greeting someone?" Human nature being what it is (see the discussions of the allegedly symbolic meaning behind the pleats in a hakama or in the colors of belts), a back-formation "explanation" would eventually evolve.

"Well, by saying 'Morning,' Americans are acknowledging that theirs is a land of opportunity, one where the promise of a new day always brings new hope and renewed optimism." Inevitably, there would be an authoritative "explanation" of that sort. More than one. All based on an inaccurate understanding of *context*. The Myth of Osu! is, in all likelihood, similarly explicable. If this word and any others are used in your dojo, follow the custom. But be very wary of extrapolating your experience in other dojo, in other budo or Japanese arts, and in your interactions with Japanese speakers. Heigo is a specialized form of speech with its own rules and applications. You should begin your study of it by learning the vocabulary. But once learned, be aware of it in context.

10

THE TEACHER

SENSEI

What do you expect of the sensei? He is a figure that has, in some small way at least, entered the vocabulary and the imagination of the West. Thanks to movies and novels about Japan, and particularly about the fighting arts of that country, we know the word. We have, further, an image. We mix the avuncular Mr. Miyagi of *The Karate Kid* fame with a smattering of the late actor Toshiro Mifune's phlegmatic and taciturn personality. Then add a dollop of the quirky, diminutive Jedi Master Yoda. Season well with the aphoristic wisdom of the Shaolin masters of the old *Kung Fu* TV series. And, distilled, we might have as a result: the perfect sensei—at least as envisioned by those who have scant exposure to the real thing. In reality, the true sensei has perhaps a smattering of those stereotypical characteristics. More likely, he is distinguished more by his ordinariness than anything else. He tends, when not actually teaching, to blend in. And even when teaching, his manner is more apt to be understated than dramatic, gently guiding; always subtle rather than nakedly charismatic. Fortune and fate have collided in his life, affording him both a measure of technical skill and a desire—or more commonly a willingness—to share his talents with others. So he becomes, to his own surprise in most cases, far enough along the Way to be able to retrace his steps in order to assist others along the same path.

As with many other institutions with roots in traditional Japan, there is no precise equivalent in the West. Having no one quite like a sensei, we are tempted to assign definitions that are misleading or inadequate or blatantly inaccurate. Similarly, the temptation inevitably is to try to explain the sensei by defining what he is not.

The sensei is not a coach. This perplexes some. Particularly those who come from a sports background and who interpret the athleticism of the budo as, more or less, an exotic form of exercise or competition. What would such activities be without a coach?

The sensei is not a father figure. Nor is he a guru, priest, or oracle. He is not an all-knowing sage, one adorned with mystical trappings and peculiar though endearing mannerisms like eschewing contractions in his speech. He is not in possession of the simple and perfect, though often enigmatic, dose of advice for solving all of the quandaries and problems of his students. There are a number of people drawn to the Japanese budo because of frailties in the infrastructure of their own self-esteem. They come because of a need for power. Or because of a compulsion to adopt some esoteric art and philosophy because of what they feel is lacking in their own culture. All of these needs act as magnetic forces compelling more than a few to make their way to the dojo. In some instances, it is their need, real or imagined, for a guy with all the answers: Daddy. Other circumstances might have led these people to a Reverend Jim Jones or a Maharishi, or to any number of cult leaders or political figures who have always been around with promises to fill in all the gaping holes or heal the flesh wounds of our souls.

The sensei is not always wizened (nor universally wise); not always patient (nor prescient); not always technically infallible (nor invincible). What the sensei *is* is largely a product of the unique circumstances of premodern Japanese culture and civilization. These, among other forces, are what made the sensei:

• Agriculture and geography combined in Japan to evolve communities tightly interwoven, where the need for authoritarian leadership was balanced with a pronounced emphasis on members of the group, village, clan, or family, all working together. Japan has had its share of tyrants. But leadership in the small, relatively isolated communities of premodern Japan usually rested on personalities that could govern and exercise influence by meeting the responsibilities that allowed the group to continue and prosper.

• Japan borrowed one form of writing from China and created their own, complementary syllabaries, both beautiful, but neither conducive to rapid or wide reproduction. Even after the introduction of the printing press to Japan, information was not easily accessed via the written word. Lacking a widespread availability of texts or other printed sources, a method for reliably imparting knowledge or skills was vital. The role of the sensei developed, in no small part, through direct interaction with his students. His teaching was not through any kind of mass instruction. It was not accomplished with the assistance of much written material. He imparted his knowledge through *isshin-denshin,* a direct, highly individualized transmission. Isshin-denshin is the "direct passing of skills or knowledge, from one to another." It is crucial to understand, too, that the intimate imparting of skills and information has also been deemed a superior way of learning in all traditional arts in Japan primarily because more than a little of the art itself resides in the personality of the teacher.

• Confucianism, once introduced to Japan during the fourth century C.E. or possibly earlier, crossbred easily with the native Japanese predilection for the veneration of age and the respect for social order. These were expressed in firmly delineated relationships between parent and child, vassal and lord, teacher and student. Status was conferred as much by age and seniority as by ability or prowess. It is no coincidence that the literal translation of *sensei* is "the preceding generation."

In a historical perspective, the sensei can be confused with an *iemoto,* or soke, or what is best translated as a "headmaster"—either the founder of a specific ryu or the inheritor of it. In some cases, the two may be synonymous. The establishment of a ryu meant that its progenitor would of necessity have been a teacher. As ryu were passed on through successive generations, the headmaster's title was awarded through inheritance in a familial process. That kept the ryu's lineage intact, yet it may have meant in some instances that the inheritor was not necessarily the best teacher of the ryu. A sensei may have been granted the right to teach the ryu by a headmaster who, although he inherited the status that came at the top of the ryu's pyramid, either did not care to teach or recognized he did not have the talent for it. Further, teachers may have been licensed to teach through the ryu if its structure was composed in such a way that allowed those so authorized and permitted to instruct. It was the headmaster's decision. This tradition continues today in classical martial arts as well as in ryu devoted to flower arranging, Noh drama, calligraphy, and so on. It is a profoundly feudalistic institution, and not always fair or reasonable. Undeniably, however, it has worked because we still have ryu that originated hundreds of years ago, still largely intact, still being transmitted to successive generations.

In modern martial arts organizations, the senior authorities in the group most often designate the sensei. The organization may have particular standards to be met in terms of rank, time spent in training, or so on, or they may confer the ability to teach based on their knowledge of the individual. And of course, there is nothing legally preventing a person from assuming the authority for himself, for going out and opening a dojo or an academy of calligraphy or a school for any Japanese art. There isn't a Central Sensei Board of Accreditation somewhere in Japan that certifies teachers of these arts. And while the person claiming to be a teacher may have elaborate papers and other documentation "proving" he's a sensei and ratified by this organization or that, those certifications could just as easily have come from an organization he created. The point is that the title of sensei is by no means one assigned in a reliable and consistent fashion, neither in Japan nor anywhere else.

The first budo sensei undoubtedly earned their position because of practical technical skills they possessed. They had survived the battlefield experience and had the ability to transmit their talents. The few scholars who have lent their energies to research this aspect of Japanese history long assumed such early combat instruction was informal in structure. This would have been about the ninth century, when feudal lords began to assemble private armies to protect their holdings, precipitating the first massed battle in Japan. One man survived in combat, remembered how he did it, and told and showed others. No real records of that time give any evidence of teaching methods otherwise. But there are some tantalizing clues in the written scrolls documenting historical events that the teaching during this period may have been more formal and structured than we might believe. Whatever. It was the introduction of the first formal ryu devoted to combat, around the fourteenth century, that saw the role of the sensei develop in a concrete way. This introduction, incidentally, is sometimes cited as the beginning of an allegedly epicene devolution of Japan's fighting arts. The argument goes that when the best—or most successful—warriors were directly teaching—teaching methods based on their victories on the battlefield—that learning was immediate and concretely rooted in "the real thing." You were guaranteed to learn from the best because the second best was crippled or dead. It's a reasonable argument. But it is critically flawed. Even the most active or pugnacious samurai faced a combative reality not much different from that encountered by the modern soldier. How many battles, how many one-on-one encounters, might he have had in his career? Maybe a dozen or so at most. Certainly not enough, except in very extreme cases, for him to be able to objectively analyze what it was that allowed him to win. One of the most salient, extraordinary values of the ryu was that it promoted a *collective* accumulation of experience. The founder may have discovered a unique principle of combat. The history of virtually all ryu, however, reveal that his students added their own insights and amplifications on these principles; so, too, successive generations. These contributions are critical in the formation of the ryu. The exponent of the traditional ryu, then, rests not on the questionable and necessarily limited experience of one man, however talented, but rather on the experiences and revelations of many, many of those who have added to the wealth of the ryu's curriculum.

By the end of the fifteenth century the ryu dominated the pedagogy of Japanese instruction in most arts. They controlled the dissemination of these arts under the direction of a headmaster and, as we noted in many cases, with the supervision of one or more sensei.

(What about other learning? Lessons in reading and writing and mathematics and other subjects were not well organized in premodern Japan. The literacy rate during the feudal era was remarkably high. More than 90 percent of Japanese during the seventeenth century could read and write. Learning, though, came from schools run by Buddhist temples or from instruction at home. Some fiefdoms established compulsory schools, and the children of samurai and higher-ranking families were taught in formal academies. However, it was not until the early twentieth century that Japan as a country established a systematic public education, one they modeled after those in Europe.)

A few ryu were impressively large in terms of enrollment. But the typical ryu was small, confined to an isolated geographical location or to even a single political domain or village. This immediacy encouraged direct interaction between the sensei and his student. It further solidified the relationship between the two. Even in the modern budo that developed after the end of the feudal period—and even in those cases where there was a deliberate attempt to "modernize" instruction and to adopt Western methods of teaching— most students had a personal relationship with the sensei. It was not until the end of the Second World War that the numbers of practitioners in the budo dojo grew so large that the teacher would have looked out to see a "class" rather than an assembly of individually recognizable students.

Today, even a small neighborhood dojo may have so many members enrolled that the teacher does not know all of the faces he sees when he bows to commence the class. It is a radical change. (Charged by one of my sensei to begin teaching a classical martial art, I asked him how many students I ought to have. Turn your back on them during practice, he advised me. If, without looking at them, you can recognize them by the sound of their shouts and the sound their feet make as they step on the ground, you've got the right number.) Other traditional Ways, such as tea ceremony or flower arranging, face the same new paradigm. The sensei is attempting to teach arts that have feudal roots, designed to be taught to adherents who were neighbors or relatives, people with whom the teacher shared a community and a lifestyle and a psychological perspective. None of that is the case now, and so he must adopt an entirely new approach. What this says about the future of these arts is by no means clear. To be certain, it has meant significant changes in the definition and role of the sensei in traditional arts.

In Japan, *sensei* as a title is used with some regularity. Schoolteachers are called sensei by their students and by society in general, given the fairly exalted status teaching has in Japan. Artists, writers, and those outstanding in their professions or talent are often called sensei. The word is even used in a jocular sense. A young man successful with women might be known, with some sarcasm intended, as "sensei" as a tribute to his romantic accomplishments. In the dojo, the word is reserved usually for the person who is the senior instructor. In a large training hall, there might be senior students whose duties may include some instruction, but they are generally not called sensei. That title is reserved for the person at the very top. All others may be thought of as seniors or instructors-in-training.

Some dojo have a variety of titles such as *renshi, kyoshi, shidoin,* and others, that designate some position of authority. Some of these titles originated in the military chain of command of the samurai. They were adopted for the modern budo by the Butokukai, an organization we noted in the chapter on the keikogi. The Butokukai originally issued ranks of renshi and kyoshi *very* sparingly. For example, the single most noted figure in Japanese karate in the twentieth century, Gichin Funakoshi, was awarded a kyoshi rank in 1943. (The president of the Butokukai at that time, incidentally, was Hideki Tojo, the prime minister and ultimate military commander of Japan's forces, who was executed as a war criminal after the end of hostilities.) After the war, these titles were first adopted by the national kendo organizations in Japan and later by some other budo forms. The standards for them were relaxed considerably. Even so, they are not easy to earn in legitimate budo circles. A title of *hanshi* is issued in kendo today after one has been named a kyoshi for at least a decade, is over the age of fifty-five, and has attained an eighth dan in the art. These titles, by the way, are almost never used in addressing the person owning them. One does not say, "Suzuki-renshi, could you help me with this technique?" No, he is addressed as "Suzuki-san" or "Suzuki-sensei." The preoccupation with these titles and their use in normal conversation in and out of the dojo is one of the characteristics of some Western dojo where, unfortunately, titles and rank are afforded far more emphasis than they are worth. But no matter what titles may be used in the dojo, there is only one sensei.

(An exception to the above would be in cases like the old Japan Karate Association or the current Aikikai headquarters of aikido, places where more than one teacher assumes responsibility for different classes during the training week. In these instances, there may be multiple sensei, each with his own students, sharing space. In these situations, it would not be inappropriate to address each of these as sensei.)

Among the more senior Western teachers of budo are several who do not allow students to refer to them as sensei. They may permit this when actual instruction is going on the in dojo, asking that at all other times they be addressed by their first name. This is a thoughtful approach, with much to recommend it. These teachers are reacting not only to the misappropriation of the word, but to the connotations it carries. To many in the West, as we've already noted, *sensei* is a title barely indistinguishable if at all from *master*. In everyday parlance, if you explain to a Japanese that Mr. Smyth is a budo sensei, they are likely to understand that Smyth is in charge of instructing others in some form of combat, period. If you make the same explanation to many Westerners, they are far more apt to infer that Smyth is an expert in the art of hand-to-hand mayhem, the possessor of near-supernatural skills, whose disciples address him only in hushed tones. That's an exaggeration perhaps. But not much. *Sensei* as a title carries all kinds of baggage here that it does not when used in Japan. Many Western teachers, wishing to avoid that kind of thing, opt instead to be addressed more informally. In other words, to return to the question with which we began this discussion, they know there are expectations of a "sensei" in non-Japanese martial arts circles. Some of these expectations are quite preposterous. Some would be impossible as criteria for any mortal to meet.

If we want a clear and accurate picture of the sensei, one way to bring it all into focus is to review those energies I mentioned above that created him.

Authoritarian leadership. The sensei is the boss. The dojo is not and can never be a democracy. It may be drastic to think of it, but in some ways the dojo is like a small boat, filled with passengers and out at sea. Think of those proto-Hawaiians, the intrepid Polynesians who left their home islands in their long, outrigger *waka* to found a new civilization in the middle of the Pacific. Anthropologists, along with Hawaii's oral traditions, tell us these canoes were captained by leaders whose orders and decisions were, by necessity, absolute law. In such extreme circumstances, where lives were on the line, there could not be votes on the size of food rations or a communal decision on who would stand watch when. For the safety of the entire canoe and the success of the voyage, authority had to come from one person. His word had to be final. In the dojo, while the circumstances are not so dire, danger is constantly present. Even in the best of circumstances, accidents can happen when people are swinging weapons at one another or hitting or kicking or throwing one another around. Emotions can be heightened in the face of such threats, even if there are safeguards in the form of rules or boundaries. For there to be coherence, order must be maintained absolutely, and there must be no question about who enforces it.

When we talk about the danger in the dojo, not incidentally, we are speaking not just of the physical threats that are always inherent when people are engaged in violent, antagonistic activities. Conflict has reverberations emotionally and psychologically. There will be the student who is dealing with a history of abuse, and another who has learned to interact with others through aggression and intimidation. There will be those tempted to use training as an opportunity for seduction or romance and who might take advantage of the environment there. The sensei is not a therapist. The goal of the dojo is to make healthy people healthier, physically and psychologically and spiritually. It cannot be expected to repair badly damaged human beings. And so if a member exhibits serious personal problems, the sensei's job is to get rid of him, gracefully if possible, forcefully and definitively if necessary. But he must also have the maturity and insight to deal with the foibles of our species. This requires leadership. It is a kind of leadership not all that different from that of the village or family leader of old, rural Japan.

In a less dramatic way, chaos can also result if the source of instruction is varied or indeterminate. The sensei is the template. The sensei must also be a leader in the sense of serving as a technical model for others. He is, properly, the *only* source of instruction. Want a fast-track exit from a traditional dojo? Approach the sensei with, "Well, I read a book that said you were supposed to do the technique this way." Or, "So-and-so does the technique that way." "Fine," you will be told. "Go study with that book or this So-and-so." When you come to the dojo, it is a recognition the teacher there has something you want. He will give it to you in his own way. You must accept that. If you do not, you are free to leave. The dojo, however, is never run by consensus.

All this talk of leadership and bosses is not to imply the sensei is a dictator. This is another example of when comparisons are inadequate, when definitions leave a gap in understanding. The sensei is the head of the dojo and the source for instruction. Yet like the leader of a family or a village, his status depends upon the loyalty of those under him. If the sensei is to be the arbiter of technical standards, then his own standards must be worthy of that position. Age or the debilitations that come with it might compromise his skills in some ways. Even so, he must be the model and it is his evaluation of skill that must be final.

That the sensei is a model, the standard for the art he teaches, explains much about the second contributing factor in Japan's cultural development of the role of the sensei: the direct imparting of skills. As we noted, the lack of published materials influenced the preference for one-on-one instruction in early Japan. Beyond this, however, was the inclination for immediacy, for a relationship between the teacher and the taught that went beyond the normal pedagogical give-and-take we expect in education. In classical ryu, the headmaster represents more than just the sole source of the curriculum. He does not merely teach the mechanics of the ryu. He is, in a very real way, the embodiment of the ryu itself. The ryu may be thought of as a unified body. Its members share lore and traditions, along with a particular perspective on things, and a technical ability. (That is another critical reason why the ryu is not easily adapted to dissemination on a mass scale.) All of this comes from one place: the headmaster. From technical details like the way he handles a weapon or comports his body to his responses to life in general, the student will reveal something of the headmaster in himself, provided he has trained long enough and been trained correctly one-on-one with that headmaster. He is not a mirror of his teacher; the goal of the ryu is not to produce clones. So much of the ryu is within the personality of its leader, however, that some degree of this transference is inevitable.

Of course, as ryu began to grow in size, this immediacy may have been compromised or lost altogether. There are ryu devoted to flower arranging or the tea ceremony, for instance, that number well into the thousands of members, spread all over the planet. A student of an ikebana ryu may have trained under his or her teacher for a decade or longer and never even laid eyes on the ryu's headmaster. Similarly, in modern martial Ways, the role of the headmaster has almost universally been deliberately replaced with a board or group of senior authorities. These leaders in turn designate senior members below them to serve as teachers who may head their own suborganizations in different countries or states or regions. Those teachers will appoint some of their senior students to run individual dojo. It is more like a corporation than the feudal family or clan model presented by the classical ryu. And it represents another major change in the relationship between a student and a teacher. If I, for instance, am training in an aikido dojo in a small town in southern Illinois, my teacher will not be, in most cases, someone who learned directly from aikido's founder or from his son or his grandson. He probably will not even have been to Japan at all. He will be the student of someone senior, maybe in Chicago or another Midwestern city large enough to have an aikido school big enough to support a teacher higher up in the seniority of aikido in the U.S. And that person, in turn, will have a teacher of higher rank and experience. Now, once or twice a year I might attend a training seminar or a camp that allows me to be on the same mat, along with dozens or even hundreds of my fellow students, being taught by my teacher's teacher's teacher. But I would not think of that man or woman as *my* teacher. My teacher is the guy who instructs me at our dojo there in Illinois.

In this kind of training situation, which is the commonest everywhere in the world today in the modern budo, I am apt not to think of my teacher as the "model" for my art. He may be only slightly senior to me, in fact. I do not look at him as the final authority on technique, even though I will accept him as the authority within our dojo. If he demonstrates a technique for me, I may say, "Well, but I saw Ishi-sensei do it this way and at that seminar he specifically said he wanted it done that way." The competent teacher will have one of two responses, both of them legitimate. He may say, "Yes, that is correct. However, at your level, I need you to do the technique as I have instructed for reasons you may not understand right now." Or, he may say, "You're right; I'd forgotten that. Let's do it as Ishi-sensei wants us to." He may also become irritated or angry at this "challenge" to his status. He doesn't realize it, but he is reverting to the response of the classical ryu's sensei or headmaster. Big difference, though. He is not a member of a classical ryu. He is not teaching in that manner and he does not have the final authority that a sensei or headmaster in a koryu in that situation would have. He is a member of a modern budo organization, one with a leader whose job it is to set standards. His job is to try to meet those standards and if you refer to them, having been given instruction in them by the leader of your organization, he ought to be grateful to you. The failure to understand this enormous difference in a modern budo organization and a classical martial ryu is one of the sadder aspects of the budo today.

While the sensei in today's dojo may not sit as absolute authority of the sort we would find in a training hall for the feudal era arts, and while his personality may not necessarily embody the spirit of the art as the ryu's sensei does, that does not preclude the vital importance of one-on-one teaching. Like any intricate or complicated art, budo has so many subtleties, so many individualized manifestations, that there is no way it can be taught through books or video or through a teacher standing at the front of a big hall and counting movements like a drill sergeant. The relationship must be immediate, at least for those practitioners seeking to move further along the Way than just the first steps. There is no other satisfactory method by which to accomplish this arduous journey than by submitting oneself to a qualified sensei and then trusting him to lead.

The final creative impetus we noted in the development of the sensei was through the contributions of Confucianism. This is a gross oversimplification. Confucianism as a philosophy and a basis for government was so readily adopted in Japan because in so many ways it was sympathetic to and consistent with indigenous concepts involving ancestor worship and social hierarchy. One of the most problematic concerns of modern budo organizations lies in their bureaucracy. Historians of budo often focus on the remarkable technical vivification offered by early modern masters like Kano, Ueshiba, and Funakoshi. But they often overlook the fertile growth of the modern budo in the newly adopted models of business organizations introduced from the West to Japan. The internal composition of a corporation that guided big business in Japan during the early part of the twentieth century had a dramatic effect on the budo as well. The feudal structure that dominated in the teaching of martial arts during the premodern era was, as we've noted, entirely pyramidal in shape. Authority issued directly from the top, descending, through a series of licenses, to teachers who were under the umbrella of the headmaster's control. This worked for the ryu as a whole and, in those cases where they existed, in the individual dojo or groups training under the immediate direction of a sensei. (We can think of this as a pyramid built entirely of rows of smaller pyramids. My loyalty is to my direct teacher; to a lesser extent to *his* teacher, and so on.)

What functioned so effectively within the classical ryu and within most crafts was not so successful within the environment of early modern Japan, however. Japanese of the Meiji and Taisho periods (1868–1926) vigorously rejected many feudal institutions. We might think of the samurai walking down the street, his two swords stuck in his belt, as a dashing and appealing figure. To generations of Japanese who had lived under the strict laws of the Tokugawa shogun, the samurai was one more hateful symbol of oppression. (The moving scene of a young samurai having his topknot forcibly cut by soldiers in the movie *The Last Samurai* needed some serious social context. The soldiers doing the cutting were drawn from the ranks of commoners who had every reason to resent a class that had lorded it over them—had literally the power of life and death over them—and who for hundreds of years lived on the taxes and toil of the lower castes.) The "old schools" of martial arts, which currently enjoy a romantic élan in the imagination of many who have read about them, were in many cases vestiges of a cruel and despotic past. Additionally, unionism was on the rise in Japan at this time. So was the suffrage movement, and a number of other egalitarian impulses. The budo were deeply affected by this spirit. Teachers like Funakoshi, Ueshiba, and Kano consciously rejected the pyramid structure that characterized teaching in the ryu. They deliberately adopted a more democratic and corporate model in the way they organized their teaching. Largely due to their personalities, they remained at the top of their schools: visible figureheads. But increasingly during the twentieth century, the responsibilities for teaching and representing the modern budo fell to a coterie of senior instructors within the art. The authority to promote was granted to these men and they often, especially after the Second World War, left Japan to begin teaching in countries all over the world. This led to serious changes and compromise in terms of the Confucian-based emphasis on a relationship of loyalty and duty to one's seniors that characterized classical systems of combat in Japan.

Today, the sensei is often caught between feudal, classical notions and contrasting modern concepts about his role and status. Unintentionally or not, he may in certain situations adopt a pose or attitude more appropriate to the headmaster of a seventeenth-century ryu, an unquestioned exemplar whose word is the final one. The same sensei, in another situation, may be the very model of democratic leadership, generous in allowing his senior students to make decisions about the group, encouraging the voting of officers within the organization, and so on. He may even rationalize this contradictory behavior in one way or another. Even so, it will inevitably lead to serious problems in the dojo. On a larger scale, entire budo organizations with worldwide membership have been irretrievably splintered when the sensei at the top cannot reconcile within himself these different approaches. Ironically, those organizations most successful in adopting corporate and democratic structures have presented the most problems for teachers in them. The sensei tries to be both a leader with unquestionable authority and simultaneously an officer of the organization who serves only with the approval of his students. Critics of modern budo lament its over-commercialization and other, tawdry aspects that characterize it all too often nowadays. The poorly understood role of the sensei in these budo, though, is a concern every bit as significant.

It would not be appropriate or realistic to conclude a discussion of the sensei in completely pessimistic terms. For several hundred years, his role has been an essential one in transmitting Japanese arts. If it is a position ripe for misuse, it is also one equally pregnant with potential. The relationship between a serious student and a mature and competent teacher in any art is enormously rewarding for both. Particularly so, the budo offer a challenging environment for these two to create something special and to preserve teachings and techniques that have been around a very long time. The sensei teaches not because he has to, but because he can. The student learns for the same reason. They are both on the same road. The sensei has gone ahead a little further—or maybe a lot—and has come back to be a guide for his student. As he walks the same path once again, not as a first-time traveler but now as one who leads another, he sees a different journey, or at least he sees it through different eyes. Both teacher and student are enriched in the process.

True, if the person claiming to be a sensei is susceptible to the crippling, degenerative effects of ego (and too small and fragile an ego can stunt as surely as one too large and obdurate), the position of teaching others has endless possibilities for abuse. For those psychologically healthy and able, though, leading others in the budo is a daily exercise in keeping the inner blade of one's self sharp and polished. There have always been individuals in Japan's budo willing to undertake this task, no matter how arduous and often thankless it is. As they are transformed through teaching others, they serve as an inspiration to another generation. Perhaps that is another, more subtle meaning in the word *sensei:* he is from the "generation preceding," as the characters for writing the word imply. The sensei is, as well, a constant and invigorating source for the creation of the generation that will follow.

II

MONEY
OKANE

There are those—I am doubtless among them—who seem to talk and write about the budo as if the martial Ways are above the mundane and grubby world of commerce: arts pursued for their aesthetic joy and quite divorced from any impure thoughts of money. This is an almost completely ridiculous notion. The operation of a dojo, even if it is in private hands, is not without expenses. There are some big ones, in fact. Just as with any other building, roofs need replacing, the plumbing malfunctions, walls need repainting. If the space is rented or being paid for with a loan or mortgage, there will need to be funds each month for that. Some training areas are located in local YMCAs or other such public or semipublic facilities, and so expenses are kept to a minimum. But it is extremely unusual that you will have access to a dojo that is "free."

Further, it is irresponsible to suggest that one's own budo practice will be cheap. When I began budo in the late sixties, the very best judo or karate uniforms made cost less than the price you can now expect to pay for a belt for a uniform today. But even then, they cost. Training equipment, travel

for special practices, fees for visiting teachers or seminars—
all these have to be expected as a part of your budo. And in
many instances, the teacher may be making either all or part
of his income through his instruction, so there will be dues
assessed for that as well. By way of vocabulary, monthly fees
for training are *gessha*. Money paid for seminars or to guest
instructors are usually politely called *sharei* or *o-rei,* both of
which mean "thanks," with the implication being that the
thanks is in the form of a remuneration.

Some will be disillusioned—even shocked—that the martial arts sensei makes a buck through his teaching. As I've
noted on the chapter about him, people can have an ideal-
ized view of the budo teacher. Often they would prefer to
think he is motivated entirely by a love for the art and a
sincere wish to pass it along and so why profane the whole
thing by money? In some dojo, the sensei participates in this
farce. Fees are discreetly slipped under the door or otherwise
indirectly and the whole matter of dues is mentioned only
obliquely if at all. Of course, in other places, making money
seems to be the sole objective of the teacher. There are
monthly fees, testing fees, seminar fees; it goes on and on,
and all of the prices are put up on the wall like a menu, as
though one were in a deli and ordering lunch. In a serious
dojo, there is usually a compromise between the financially
oriented mentality of the merchant and that of the ascetic
warrior who is beyond the tawdry concerns of lucre. But
money is always a factor. It has always been so. During the
feudal era, there were professional instructors in the martial
arts. They were either paid as independent contractors or

received a stipend for their teaching as a part of their salary from the lord by whom they were retained. Much has been made of the supposed fact that the samurai was "above" money and was actually prohibited from carrying or using it. The warrior class was prohibited at various times in Japanese history from engaging in commerce. But of course he received a salary, usually in the form of a stipend. Still, this image of the samurai and his disdain for money is a strong one, even among modern Japanese. It undoubtedly contributes to the assumption that a sincere pursuance of the budo implies one ought never to be concerned about money.

Money becomes a problem and an impediment to the dojo when it becomes the *primary* concern—when it and not the furtherance and perfection of the art becomes paramount. There are those teachers who look upon the budo or other Asian combative arts as a business and who approach it from that standpoint. Decisions about class size, about schedules for classes, about who will be allowed to train: when these are based on making a profit, other considerations that ought to be more important tend to be pushed aside or neglected. Teaching, whether it is in front of a kindergarten class or in a pottery studio or before a dojo full of budoka, is not a normal job. Even if one is well paid, the motivation for teaching others, for sharing knowledge, must emanate from a deeper stimulus. You should be able to ascertain fairly quickly if this is present in a budo sensei. It is impossible to hide one's enthusiasm for teaching others; it is equally difficult to conceal it if one's real motivation is making a profit.

12

THE STUDENT

DESHI

The student. You. A student, in Japanese, is a *gakusei*. It is a word usually used to denote those enrolled in some formal educational institution, from kindergarten to graduate school. For the traditional arts, the student is more apt to be called a *deshi*. It's written with the characters for "younger brother" and "child." The implication is that the student is more than just a body in a classroom, more than simply a person in search of learning some skill or art. *Deshi* implies one is part of a family or at least seeks to join. There is something less formal about the word *deshi* in comparison with *gakusei,* something altogether appropriate within the context of the traditional budo. *Shoshinsha* is another word—a "person with a beginning mind"—that can describe the new student. The wise student remains a shoshinsha all during his training in the martial Ways, always with a mind that is ready to learn more and always ready to accept that he has not seen it all, no matter how much experience and talent he may gain.

The word I like best, especially when referring to a new or

prospective student, is *monjin*. One of the particular beauties of writing in kanji, in symbols that can convey more than just sounds but are composed originally of thoughts or things, is that we can break down the characters and reflect on their etymology. In the case of *monjin,* the two kanji for writing it mean "a person at the gate." The image is evocative. And apt. The person standing at the entrance to the dojo for the first time is standing at a threshold. It will be entirely up to him, in the long or short run of it, how far past the gate he goes. There is no way, looking at him, to tell. The most ambitious and excited of students at the gate or those who look to be the most physically fit may never make it past the first couple of steps before boredom or life's circumstances or the quick realization that this stuff ain't for him prevents him from going further. Conversely, the person who is tentative, who insists he only wants to peek in and have a look around, may well be the one who is there training decades later, completely immersed in the art. But all of them, all of those standing at the gate, will have reason to pause, just as you and I did, to consider how we happened to be here.

How did you get to this place? Maybe you found it upon the suggestion or recommendation of a friend, or looked for it in a phone book. Maybe you found it on a Web site. What, though, got you to that point? It is a fascinating question: what brings a person to the budo? Curiosity plays a role. And there is the draw of the exotic. The lure of promised power, as we've mentioned before, is a strong attractive device for some. *Hosshin* is a word sometimes used to describe the moti-

vation in a person drawn toward the budo or to some other
art of equal profundity. It usually refers to a religious awaken-
ing or a conversion of the spirit. It can also mean, as it does
in this context, the turning over of a new leaf. The would-be
budoka realizes something is missing in his life. It could be
that he wants to be stronger, to be able to defend himself in
any violent situation. He may have seen extraordinary feats
performed by "masters," or he may have had a romantic attraction to the traditional arts because of a movie or book
that featured them. And maybe, as with so much in life, he's
at the gate because "it just seemed like a good idea at the
time."

If you are to proceed past the gate, you will find that the
path beyond is unexpectedly steep and narrow, at least at the
beginning. It is so tight and so acutely pitched, in fact, that
there is no room for much of what you have that you think
you need to take along. This can be a daunting realization. It
can be so frightening that most of those who are at the gate
of a traditional dojo will not make it very far at all. They are
so heavily weighed down with what they fervently believe
they must have that they can't make the journey. In some
cases, these items are trivial if we look at them objectively.
For example, a young man might come to the dojo believing
he is going to become a "samurai." That he will be learning
the art taught there in a way similar to scenes of martial arts
practice in period dramas or movies. Obviously, his glowing
perceptions of an ancient time that for the most part did not
exist in the reality of historical Japan will be in glaring con-

trast to what actually goes on in a dojo. But if he can't let go of his preconceptions, he can't make it through. In other instances, the belongings newcomers try to bring through the gate are of a more serious nature. A woman who has been sexually abused might come to believe that budo will empower her or substitute for therapy. There are in the world a number of injured souls, those with holes in their personalities or emptiness in their hearts, and some of them inevitably, having heard or read of the spiritual values of the budo, will end up standing at the gate. The cold truth is that while serious budo has remarkable and deep spiritual aspects, it is not a form of counseling or a religion. It cannot repair souls or complete personalities or fill hearts. It is cruel and misleading for some dishonest or inadequately trained teachers to suggest otherwise. The would-be student who tries to get past the gate because he expects that beyond it will be a therapist or a support group or a place of worship will be disappointed. Ultimately he will fail because what he seeks isn't there.

Assuming he is healthy—mentally, morally, and physically—and that he is willing to approach the path in front of him for what it is and not for what he would like it to be, most individuals have little trouble getting past the gate and entering the dojo. There might be the perception that what goes on in a traditional dojo is severe, that it is the equivalent of Special Forces training and that only the strong will survive within it. This notion is reinforced by mention of *shugyo,* a word often used in describing budo training. It means "austere training." It has a ring of the elite and the demanding about it. The first time he hears of it, the student might have images of various mortifications of the flesh, mysterious rituals of auto-de-fé, a willingness to submit to all manner of rigorous testing of body and spirit. Indeed, tales of the dojo are replete with challenges like facing one hundred opponents in contests that do not end for hours and hours, or fighting one's way through a maze studded with perilous traps or hidden opponents who leap out to attack. (More often than not, it will be explained to the credulous that these were once a part of training but have been discontinued now because no one training in the art today is up to it. No matter when you start your tenure in a martial Way, you can be assured that it was much, much tougher in "the old days," that period being most accurately defined as a couple of years before you came along.)

In the long era of Japan's history in which the samurai were an important component of the civilization, the professional fighting class of men there on occasion submitted themselves to these kinds of harsh training methods. There are all sorts of stories of their adventures. They might choose to live out in the forest as hermits, practicing incessantly and communing with the *tengu,* the mythical beasts of Japan's mountains who would sometimes take an interest in or at least pity on the fortunate human and pass along the secrets of their magical combat skills. Today there are still some dojo where feats of endurance are a part of the curriculum, where members are tested in extreme situations that challenge their stamina or fortitude. These might be thought of as some kind of shugyo. More realistically, though, shugyo is a matter of making the sometimes substantial changes in one's life or daily routine in order to follow a budo. If you are serious about your training, you will not need to look for extraordinary challenges or be subjected to daunting tasks. Everyday life has its own shugyo, as you will quickly discover.

From the moment you enter a dojo as a student you enter a hierarchy. Those who have come before you, even if it is only a day before you, are your *sempai.* Two kanji are used to write the word; the first refers to something that came previously. It's the same *sen* as in *sensei.* The second, *pai* or *hai,* means "comrade." Anyone who comes to the dojo after you have begun your training is your *kohai.* The second kanji for kohai is the same as in sempai; the first means "coming after." On the odd chance that you commence your training on the same day as someone else, you will each be *dohai* to one another. (The *do* in the word is "the same" or "equal.") For the most part, though, everyone in the dojo will be either your junior or your senior.

The conventions of sempai/kohai are often explained in terms of upper and lower classmates in a school or the relationships between juniors and seniors in the work environment. In some ways they are just that simple. In others, the sempai/kohai concept is far more complex and defies any kind of easy explanation. A very good argument can be made, actually, that the notion of sempai/kohai really has no coherent way of implementation outside the context of traditional

Japanese society. In most dojo where the relationship is understood, it is, ironically, most often ignored. Except under unusual circumstances, one does not actually refer to another as his sempai or kohai in addressing him. They might say, "Bob is my sempai," but they would not approach him and say "Sempai, can you help me?" as though the title were a form of address. Sempai/kohai has its roots in the Confucian forms of social interaction that guided much of Japanese life for centuries. It is most often considered today to be a convention of the college or university world, where one has classmates both ahead and behind one while matriculating. In some universities in Japan, this relationship is more formal, especially at the more prestigious schools. In others, it has little meaning other than the appellations of "freshman" and "sophomore" might have in an American school. Businesses might also have a tradition of sempai/kohai. In these cases, one's position is established within the school or the firm. Additionally, a sempai might develop a mentoring relationship with a kohai. This is not a formal contract. For one reason or another, a junior and senior might simply get along in such a way that the latter looks out for the former, counsels him in getting along, and provides advice.

Both in Japan and outside the country, the sempai/kohai relationship can be expressed in unhealthy ways. Sometimes it emerges as something rather like that of a social fraternity where active members make the lives of pledges miserable, hazing them, ordering them about, using their seniority as an excuse to engage in behavior that often is brutal. In some university karate clubs, famous for their machismo in Japan, junior members have literally been beaten to death by seniors ostensibly seeking to "toughen them up." This is a complete perversion of classical warrior values that evolved in Japan. The cohesion of the group was all-important to a group of samurai who depended upon one another for their mutual survival. Traumatizing one's own members within the group through sadistic hazing was counterproductive to the military success of the clan. More likely, the abuse of the sempai/ kohai system in Japan, particularly at the university level, is a reflection of some of the darker aspects of Japanese society. There is in that society a fear and antagonism toward anyone "different," and the difference can be measured in myriad ways, including just being a newcomer. Further, the sense of togetherness and cohesion so important in Japan is often bizarrely reinforced by vicious exclusion. In the U.S., this kind of brutality is more likely to be expressed because the teacher has had some experience in the military (or more likely has had some experience watching military training as depicted in movies). And so he assumes the correct relationship between a senior and a junior is like that of a drill instructor and a boot camp enlistee. Possibly because the first taste many Americans had of the martial Ways of Japan was served to them by men who had learned these arts while in the U.S. military in Japan, the budo have acquired in some regards a strong flavor of that boot camp mentality just mentioned. This attitude was reinforced in some instances by Japanese instructors who came into their own when Japan was at the height of its expansionist militarism, during the thirties. The equation, in either instance, is understandable. After all, they are *martial* arts, no? Yes, they are. However—and this is absolutely critical to understanding and pursuing a budo—the martial ethos of the traditional Japanese samurai was in many, many ways, very different than that of the modern military. The samurai, with some notable exceptions, were a hereditary caste. They were not conscripts, nor, given the structure of their world, did they have to go through the process of military indoctrination that is standard and necessary in the military today. During the long periods of war in premodern Japan, no one had to tell a young man how to hold a sword in the way a new private in the Army must be told how to hold his rifle. The samurai had been doing it almost all his life. His skills were in need of refinement. But he knew how to conduct himself and how to follow orders; it was part of his culture. It would be worthwhile for the budoka to learn more about the world of the samurai and how it differed from that of the fighting man today. And it is very important to know that those who use the sempai/kohai system as a kind of "basic training" are grossly misusing the institution and for means that are, at best, questionable.

Earlier I noted that some insist the whole concept of sempai/kohai works only within the frame of Japanese society and really ought to be dispensed with outside it, especially in the dojo. Let me give an example that also illustrates another possible misuse of the system. If someone is your sempai, he is your sempai for the rest of your life. Whatever happens along the way can never change that relationship. A sempai could quit his training a month after you begin and be gone from the dojo for the next decade. If he showed up again and you were still training and had been all that time, to be sure you would be technically superior to him. Makes no difference. He would still be your sempai and would still expect you to defer to him. This creates problems in the dojo in Japan and elsewhere, as you might guess. Training halls there and here are sometimes plagued by sempai who haven't stepped onto the training floor in years but who show up one day to restart their practice and who take the attitude of the wise and experienced "old-timer" around those who are their juniors. Their conduct is both ridiculous and dangerous. No one can maintain his skills without fairly constant instruction and regular training. Just because he is "sempai" does not confer special powers on him. He'll be clumsy and slow. He will have forgotten. He will be rusty. Presumably the teacher will have improved over all that time, and so if he's good, his students will be better as well. The prodigal sempai who shows up and makes corrections and suggestions on the training floor may be drawing on lessons that have been greatly improved and refined in his absence. And so the junior is left gritting his teeth and muttering to himself, "That's not how sensei is showing it now!" and otherwise tolerating what is a hindrance to training. Not all sempai who've been out of practice for a long time will adopt this attitude. You can see, however, how the conventions of the sempai/kohai relationship can be a stumbling block in the dojo.

Within the dojo in general, sempai are expected to bring along those under them. They may push and prod and challenge their kohai to succeed and improve. Training in a dojo is not easy and the junior should expect to do a little suffering and a lot of sweating. He should also look at those ahead of him who are pulling him along and see that they are doing the same. If the behavior in a dojo between seniors and juniors falls over the line into brutality, however, one should seriously consider the wisdom in continuing to stay in such a place. As you continue to train too, you may develop a personal relationship with a senior, which is another facet of the sempai/kohai relationship. If you are serious about your practice, sooner or later it is likely you will be noticed by a sempai who will take you under his or her wing and who will explain to you, advise you, and take a personal interest in your training. This is perhaps one aspect of the sempai/kohai system that is worth preserving in the dojo and that can transcend differences in culture.

Aside from sempai and kohai, other roles in the dojo are assigned to those working as "attackers" and "defenders." Again, the nomenclature fails. You and I are practicing a technique, an armlock for example, that our teacher has just demonstrated. I approach you and make a strike for your head. You seize my arm to prevent it. I then go into the mechanics of the armlock, which you receive. From one perspective, I am the defender, since I am practicing the technique, and you are the attacker. But I initiated your response with my first strike. So who's what? There is a useful expression in the budo: *kobo ichi.* "Attack and defense are one." Observing a training session, particularly among advanced students, which one is which is often difficult to ascertain. At any rate, to distinguish the roles in some way, you will hear terms like *uke* and *nage,* or *ukete* and *semete. Uke* is from the verb *ukeru,* "to receive." In arts involving throwing or grappling, the uke will be the person thrown or successfully immobilized. *Nage* is from the verb *nageru,* "to throw." The nage is the "doer," the uke the "done to." In karate, the person assailing with the initial attack is the semete, from the verb *semeru.* He is the "attacking hand." *Ukete* means the "receiving hand," the person who successfully meets and counters the attack. In kendo circles as well as in some other arts, the person making the conclusive attack is the *shidachi;* the one receiving the attack—who is usually the one who has made the initial strike to begin the engagement as well—is *uchidachi. Shidachi* is roughly translated as "the gentleman with the sword," while *uchidachi* means "the striking sword." An opponent in general is an *aite.* The *ai* here means "mutual," while the *te* is the same as that of *karate,* meaning literally a "hand" but figuratively "a person." Sometimes an opponent will be referred to as a *teki,* an "enemy." But only in figurative terms does this word have a proper place in a dojo.

As a student, you will also encounter a number of different kinds of keiko (or *-geiko* when the word is applied as a suffix), that is, a number of ways of training. Those just introduced to the ways of the dojo may believe the teacher will stand in front of the class, explaining or demonstrating a technique, and then the class will practice it. In fact, this is a small part of training. To be sure, the teacher is the authority and should be the only person responsible for instruction. But learning takes place through the interaction with others in the dojo, with one's seniors and juniors and equals. The terminology for these three kinds of training is borrowed from kendo. But they have a direct application in all budo and they need to be kept in good balance in order for progress to be made. Please note that although I am continuing to use the words *senior* and *junior,* in discussing these three kinds of training I'm not referring specifically to sempai and kohai but rather to those who are more technically skilled and advanced and those who are comparatively less so.

Training under the guidance of a senior or more experienced dojo member is *hikitate-geiko. Hikitate* means "to pull along." The role of the senior in training when he is interacting with a junior is critical. We have just discussed some of the ways in which this manifests itself within the context of the sempai and kohai. The skills and technique of the senior are superior. He knows more about the art and knows how to apply it; in most cases he could dominate his junior if it were a real fight or contest. If he does so in practice, the junior becomes frustrated, timid, and loses any confidence he might have. It is the senior's job to ensure that does not happen. He must "pull along" the junior. In some cases this will mean allowing the junior to strike or throw or otherwise "win" in practice. The senior knows how to stifle or counter the technique being practiced, but he does not. He lets his junior get a feel for it and the opportunity to apply it. He cannot become lazy about this, however. As soon as the junior has some concept of what he's doing and has been able to make the technique work, the senior must up the pace. He must make it just slightly more difficult for the junior to perform. (If the junior becomes arrogant and cocky with his "success," the senior must shut him down completely. The junior must understand what's happened, that he's taken advantage of the senior's willingness to teach, and must change his attitude immediately.) The interaction between seniors and juniors in the dojo is a constant and dynamic one. In a matter of seconds when they begin practice, the senior must ascertain the skill level of his junior partner and adapt to it. If he's too severe and prevents the junior from any success, the interaction breaks down. If he's too lax, on the other hand, the junior does not get a realistic sense of what he's doing.

When you are in the role of the more skilled partner, remember what it was like when you were on the other side. Treating your partner with condescension or in a manner that can make him believe you are toying with him and are eager to be finished so you can go off and practice with others who can put up more of a fight is a sure sign of a senior who is that in name only. It is very difficult to train with integrity and sincerity against an opponent you know you can defeat easily. This is especially true when training with children. Treat juniors with respect, with the sense that they are significant and that their training matters. Remember too that there will be that moment, no matter how good you are, when your junior will surprise you. Those not so advanced do not have the tutored responses you expect. They will come up with something, maybe not a good technique, but it will catch you unawares. When it does, you as a senior will have another opportunity to prove you are worthy. You can acknowledge their strike or throw or whatever they have managed to inflict upon you or you can pretend it "wasn't real." You can criticize them for any flaws you might see or might wish to see, in order to maintain the position you think you have in the dojo. For a while, if you adopt this attitude, they may believe you. The budo, though, have a way of revealing the truth about many things, not the least of which is the truth about ourselves. Very quickly your junior will see through the pose and perceive that your self-image and status are more important than his learning.

Kakari-geiko, or "attack practice," is the kendo term for training with one who is senior to you. Again, it applies to every form of budo, however. While the responsibility for setting the pace and intensity of the practice is up to the senior, the junior has his own duties when training with a senior. He must never take undue advantage of the fact that he's being given an opportunity to make his techniques work. Kakari-geiko is a time to try out newly learned lessons. It is not an opportunity to show off or to try to impress your senior. He's giving you a chance to try to perfect your art. Take it. To practice against someone you know is superior, to try your best against someone who's seen all that you have learned, has learned it as well, and has had more time to polish it than you, can be intimidating. You must also confront your self-doubts. "I made that work against him but he wasn't really trying to prevent it since he's just letting me practice," is a common thought for a junior, along with the suspicion that had this been "real," the results would have been very different. Alternately, some juniors who are successful in implementing their techniques against a senior in the dojo will immediately allow it to go to their heads, as I mentioned above. "He isn't so tough!" Additionally, the junior working with one of his senior classmates may feel there is a spotlight on him because of it and that the teacher will be watching, and so he must "perform." "If sensei sees me doing well against my senior, he's likely to give me more attention, or advance me in rank more quickly, or take me more seriously as his student," goes the thinking here.

In short, a junior working with a senior is tempted to think too much. His perceptions are loaded with doubts about his own abilities or exaggerated estimations of them; all these sorts of ideas will clog the free flow of his technique. Instead, he should focus, when working with a more skilled opponent in the dojo, on one thing: what can this sort of training teach me? He should get rid of his ego, his worries about performing well or his pride in having done so, and simply learn. Be open to what the senior is trying to show you, both in his explicit instruction and in the more subtle, implicit lessons he's demonstrating.

Training with an equal, or *gokaku-geiko,* presents its own

challenges. It is natural in the dojo as well as in other places where people gather for a purpose for them to establish some kind of pecking order. When training with someone who is your equal, more or less, there is the temptation to try to be just a little bit better in order to improve your own standing (as you perceive it) in the dojo. If the dojo is not a mature and healthy one, you might do this with some success. Natural talent or physical prowess or sheer determination might carry you to a level where those who have begun their training in the dojo at the same time as you are no match for you technically. This may impress a teacher who isn't fully cognizant of his role and who will be happy to have such an outstanding student. A good teacher in a good dojo, however, will understand that skill in the budo tends not to advance at a fixed rate. Sooner or later, given the nature of a budo, all those who follow it will run into periods when they don't seem to be able to improve. Fellow trainees you were able to defeat rather easily a few months ago are now handling you with little problem, much to your considerable frustration. What happened? What happened was that some of them were in a period of their training where you were months before, making rapid progress when others in the class were stalled. Now it's your turn. And now the skilled teacher will begin to watch you. He wasn't impressed by your abilities when they suddenly zoomed beyond those of your classmates; he's seen it before. What he wants to see is how well you will handle it when your training hits one of those long, slow spots where any improvement seems years away and where you cannot seem to get anywhere no matter how or what you try.

Gokaku-geiko, therefore, has to be put in perspective. *Gokaku* means "even" or "evenly matched." But even if you began training the same day as your friend and even if you have both attended and practiced with the same consistency and intensity, rarely will you be truly "equal." With that in mind, use gokaku-geiko as an opportunity to try techniques or strategies that are difficult for you. When you are training with a junior, you must be careful not to overwhelm him or to present such an intimidating opposition that he is discouraged. When you are facing a senior, your first priority must be to learn from him. When training with an equal, you can forget about both these responsibilities and simply try to put into practice all that you know. If you have a technique that does not work well for you and another that is just the opposite, opt for the former. Against an opponent of more or less equal skill and experience, you have a chance to see what you are doing wrong in a relatively realistic environment. You can polish what needs polishing. When you train with one of your equals, use it as a time to try something different. Do not look at gokaku-geiko as a *shiai,* or competition. If he is better than you on this evening's training and scores more against you or performs the techniques being taught better, next week it may be you who are succeeding. And if not next week, then next year. All the budo are full of aphorisms about the inconsequential nature of winning or losing. Gokaku-geiko is where one truly experiences this. It is a moment in your training when you can be free to employ all that you know and to explore the limits of your skills.

In addition to the three basic encounters for training in the dojo, there are other terms you might hear that relate to regular practice. *Jiyu-renshu* is one. It means "free practice," and is a period where one may move around, training with various members of the dojo informally, with no "lesson" being taught. Another similar term is *godo-geiko*. *Godo* in Japanese means "joint," or "combined," or "united." *Godo-geiko* usually refers to a practice session in which two or more related dojo get together to share an informal practice. There is little if any teaching or instruction at a godo-geiko. Instead, it is a time to exchange experience through training with others who are not regular practice partners.

You might hear people talk about *shido-geiko,* which means "to train through teaching." When you have been at the dojo for a while, the teacher will eventually give you some responsibility for introducing new material or for overseeing the practice of your juniors. You will be astonished when this happens. What you thought you knew and understood very well will, when you try to translate it to students, suddenly become foreign and complex in ways you never imagined. They will have questions about it you never thought to ask. They will present problems you never encountered and so have difficulty in addressing. It is gratifying to be thought competent enough by your teacher to be given the responsibility for instructing, even in a limited way. It will soon, however, be very, very humbling. Look forward to shido-geiko, not for the chance it affords you to show others what you know but rather for the opportunity it presents you in seeing how much you have left to learn.

Jishu-geiko and *tandoku renshu* are terms for "solitary practice." (*Sotai renshu* refers to any kind of paired practice.) These do not refer to any specific method; they merely indicate a period of activity in the dojo. If the teacher announces it is time for tandoku renshu, he means you should do some of the solo training exercises taught in the dojo. Another kind of keiko is *me-geiko* or *mitori-geiko*: training by watching. If you have become hurt or ill or if you've been training and become tired and need a brief rest, you may find yourself sitting off to the side. If it is an illness or injury that prevents your full participation, you are well enough to come to the dojo but you cannot physically train. The time can be frustrating. One wants badly to be back on the floor, but common sense or a doctor's orders or a combination of both indicates otherwise. When this happens, use the time to your advantage. Watch. You will see many things from an entirely different perspective when you are off to the side. You will see others making mistakes you make. You will see—watch for this—the teacher patiently correct a student only to have that student make exactly the same mistake only a few minutes later. The budo are remarkably complicated arts on one level. There is too much to absorb all at once. Correct the position of my feet, and my hands will be in the wrong place. Correct my arm position, and my feet will be right back in the wrong place. In the training of the classical martial arts it is an axiom that giving more than two corrections or instructions in a single training session is a waste, since the student cannot comprehend and usefully absorb much more than that at any one time. You will see even more advanced practitioners making errors. Of course, you will also see those who are doing things better than you, and you can see in many cases, if you watch carefully, how they are doing it. It should be obvious that learning by watching is not a satisfactory way to train on a consistent basis. The budo demand participation. Yet from time to time it is valuable to "look in" on what's going on in the dojo, where there is always a different, and in some ways more valuable, view than what one sees while actually training in it.

Although it is not typically thought of as such, *shinsa,* or testing for grades in the budo, is still another kind of practice. Much has been made of the system of ranking, usually through the awarding of different colored belts (discussed in detail in the chapter on the keikogi), called the dan-i method of grading. For some, this is a stressful time, particularly if the dojo makes it a formal event in which those to be graded must demonstrate before the teacher or a board of seniors. Experiencing anxieties at the thought of performing in front of others is natural. But you need to see it for what it is. Testing is a matter of evaluation. You are not the first person to have undergone this evaluation. No matter how good or bad you are, it is unlikely you are going to show the teacher anything he hasn't seen before. If you pass the testing, that's nice. If you fail, that's not so bad. You are in this for the long haul, remember. There will be other gradings. You will pass some of them and probably fail others. If you are not involved in the budo for that long haul—if you are in the dojo only because you want to get a black belt or for some other easily achievable goal—then you aren't going to last long. And so, when considered over the course of many, many years, the failure or success at a single grading is rarely a momentous occasion.

As a student, a monjin, a person at the gate, this idea that there isn't going to be a graduation or a goal to be reached may be the most important lesson for you to learn. It is a difficult one to really absorb. Some will not be able to do it at all. The notion that you will just continue to do this thing again and again, week after week, year after year, is too foreign, too odd, and from a modern perspective in many instances, too nonsensical. If you are about to join a dojo or if you have been a member for a while, look around. There will be lots of people there. Some of them you will like. Some of them you will like a lot. But chances are, they will not all be here this time next year. Some will move on to other things. Some will drop out for a variety of reasons. We say that we are engaged in following a Way. Think of it as a long climb in the mountains. There will be some of your companions who will lack the strength or the capacity to live at the higher altitudes you will be required to climb. There will be others who will be happy when they have reached a certain elevation. They have gone high enough and do not wish to go further. Bidding them farewell, if you plan to go further, is an enormously difficult thing to do. It may cause you to question your own journey. Are they the smart ones for giving it up and moving on to something else?

Earlier, we talked about hosshin, about the sense within that led us to the gate. People generally have interesting stories about how they began the budo. When you ask them not why they began but rather why they continue to stay, however, most will have difficulty answering. Why have they stayed when others have quit? What is it that keeps them coming to the dojo? There is no easy answer to these questions. That may be because at their core, the budo excite within us an inner dialogue. They pose challenges, make demands, exact sacrifices that, while we may never discuss them, are often consciously and unconsciously on our minds as we progress. These questions may not have answers, in fact. The time will come when, satisfactorily answered or not, they cease to concern us so much. We follow our Ways because they are, in the Japanese vernacular, *boku michi*—"our way." We cannot imagine *not* following the paths along which they have led us. At that point, some might consider us as having "mastered" our budo. We have not. What we have done is gone through the gate. We have become students.

13

THE DOJO YEAR

If you live within walking distance of your dojo you should consider yourself blessed. It is convenient, of course, to have such easy access to a place where you spend so much time. As importantly, however, and maybe even more so, is that by walking to the dojo for your practice and then walking home again afterward, you are allowed some moments to "decompress." You have a stretch of time mentally to go from the demands of your work or your schooling or whatever's going on in your home or your life, to your training. Once completed, the walk home serves as a way of getting you back in touch with life outside the dojo. Even if it is a drive or a train ride to and from the dojo, this intermediary space in your day is valuable. It is also pleasant if the walk or the ride takes you outside, to encourage you to think, even if for a moment, about the seasons that are constantly changing around us.

Japan, like the United States, is fortuitously situated on the planet so that each of the seasons is felt and seen easily. The old, original calendar for the Japanese was broken into twenty-four periods of about a couple of weeks each, each with its own name that reflected nuances of change within the seasons. The *Shosho,* or "manageable heat," period of late August was followed by the period of *Hakuro,* or "white dew," that marked the beginning of autumn. This sensitivity to the passing of time and to the changes wrought during the evolution of the natural year is a hallmark of Japanese literature such as haiku, and of many, many aspects of traditional arts there. It may seem odd that it would have any place in budo. I would be hard-pressed to make a convincing argument that one's technique will markedly improve by paying close attention to the season outside the dojo. I could not prove in any statistical way that walking to or from your dojo on a regular basis will have a measurably salutary effect on your understanding of what it is you are doing when you are at that dojo. Still, there are factors in the maturation of the budoka that are not so easily measured. Even if you do not find the notion persuasive, file it away and rethink it when a few years have passed. For the time being, you will need to be cognizant of the seasons or at least the calendar, because events unfold in the yearly life of the dojo that are celebrated, or at least recognized. If you are a part of the place, then as a member you will be expected to participate in most, if not all, of them.

We begin at the end, in a way, during the last weeks of December, when preparations begin for the celebration of the coming new year. . . .

Where only weeks before, the trainees at the dojo were perspiring in the last, stifling days of summer, frost has now whitened the countryside, and the floor of the training hall, especially in the mornings, has a definite chill. Thick keikogi uniforms, extra-heavyweight, are welcome now. There isn't much talk when putting them on. The students are eager to get out and warm up a bit before class starts. Winter has come again. As the dojo adjusts, its members once more prepare for that season's most important event in the training hall, called *Oshogatsu:* the celebration of the New Year.

Making ready for the new year is called *kotohajime* in Japan. In the dojo, kotohajime customarily begins on December 13. On or near this day, in addition to the daily cleaning chores in the training hall, every crack is swept, every cranny carefully dusted or cleaned. Floors and other wooden surfaces are given a polishing. Windows are thrown up to air out the place. December 13, however, is also the day when pupils of all the traditional arts dress in formal kimono and pay a visit to their masters or teachers to thank them for all their efforts. Martial artists, as well as students of pottery, tea ceremony, calligraphy, and other disciplines, present their teachers with small gifts and talk about the previous year's training. I'm sad to say that as the traditional arts grow rarer in Japan, fewer and fewer students maintain this ritual. Even though I trained in the U.S., each December I would formally give my sensei a gift of homemade chocolate chip cookies and thank him for his instruction. Nearly all the students I knew, of budo, or tea ceremony, or flower arranging, did the same. It is sad to see such institutions fade away and, while it may be impractical, serious budoka ought to try to make some effort to keep the ritual alive if possible.

The kamidana and everything on the shelf are all given a thorough cleaning as well. Usually around the twenty-seventh of December, *shogatsu shitaku* is observed, by decorating either the kamidana itself or, more typically, by erecting a table in front of it for the purpose. In some dojo this decoration can be elaborate; in others, it will be very simple. Bottles of sake, a tangerine-like fruit, and rice are displayed, along with other items with symbolic significance. The specific kind of fruit normally used is *daidai*, or bitter tangerine; written with different characters but pronounced the same it can also mean "from one generation to the next." Sprigs of *urajiro*, a kind of evergreen, grow only in pairs, and so they are a common decoration, representing fidelity in marriage or other relationships.

Yuzuriha, a tree whose old leaves fall from the branches only after the young leaves are well on their way to maturity, symbolizes the passing on of knowledge from one generation to the next, so its branches are also commonly present at the kamidana's New Year decorations. Local customs also vary widely in this regard in Japan. Around Nara, where one of my sensei was from, part of the standard dressing-up of the shelf was with strips of dried seaweed. In some places, balls of glutinous rice are skewered on branches set on or around the kamidana; in others, intricate weavings of rice straw are displayed.

In most dojo that observe some aspect of the traditional

New Year celebration, the kamidana is decorated with a fat round *kagami mochi*. Kagami mochi are cakes of a gluey paste made of pounded sweet rice, called *mochi*. Shaped into disks like round mirrors, or *kagami,* these decorations in the dojo represent the polished mirror of self-reflection into which the budoka must constantly peer to attain a true polishing of himself.

With the dojo swept clean of the old year's dust and the altar shelf laden with offerings, a new season of training is ready to begin. Today, many modern dojo in Japan shut down for the two weeks surrounding New Year's Day. The reason is more practical than ceremonial: New Year's is a fabulously busy time in Japan, with all manner of social obligations that have to be met, trips to family shrines, and so on. Few pupils would be able to make regular practice sessions. But at some traditional training halls a practice session is scheduled for the New Year's Eve, and there are dojo in the United States that have followed this custom. Often these are scheduled so first half of the practice occurs in the last hour of the old year and the final practice hour begins the new one. This training is *Toshikoshi-geiko,* literally "New Year's Eve Practice." The first complete practice of the new year is *keiko-hajime,* "beginning practice." If the dojo is closed during the first week of the year, this initial practice may not occur until after it's reopened. In the time in between, dojo may have a night of dining, drinking, and general celebration in commemoration of the start of another year. This is often called *kagami biraki.* Like the rice cake mochi in the mirror shape, *kagami biraki* refers to the same symbol. The words mean "a mirror opening." Shinto priests at the New Year often remove coverings over the mirrors that are in the heart of many Shinto shrines, and that are normally kept behind doors or otherwise concealed. Amid the frequently raucous party of the season, kagami biraki in the dojo symbolizes the same concept implied in the Shinto shrine: a pause from daily training to look deeply into one's spirit.

New Year's festivities, by the way, can be somewhat different for many koryu, or classical schools of martial art. Some of them still observe the old lunar calendar that predates both the Chinese lunar calendar and the Western Gregorian calendar that came after that. By this reckoning, the new year comes not at the dark of the moon but at the first full moon. It is called *koshogatsu,* the "little new year," and it was most often observed (and still is, in some places) in rural Japan. It makes sense, from the perspective of the farmer or other villager who lived close to nature. A full moon gave enough light to have ceremonies and other festivities in the night hours. Martial ryu that have their roots in the countryside of Japan may still observe koshogatsu. Students and teachers might gather at the home temple of the ryu or at the residence of the headmaster for a special dinner. Formal demonstrations (*hono embu*) or a special training session (*hono-geiko*) take place, meant for the spirits of the ryu's ancestors.

In many ways, the rationale behind the rituals and celebrations of Oshogatsu is in remembering and looking back. Another year of training has been completed. New members have come to the dojo; others may have been lost for one reason or another. And then another year of training begins, another season of the dojo is renewed.

Winter is also the time for *kan-geiko,* or "cold training." This takes place in what is normally the coldest part of the season in Japan, near the end of January. Kan-geiko can be a single session or it may last for a week or more. Unless the temperatures are dangerous, it often involves outside practices. *Kanchu tanren,* or "cold weather training," has long been a staple of budo. Is it masochistic? In some instances it can be. The budoka contemplating kan-geiko needs to put it in perspective. First, of course he must consider medical implications. Those suffering severe illnesses or in fragile health will need to carefully assess their participation. Kan-geiko places a lot of strain on our bodies. That said, most of us are healthy enough to train in the cold for a brief period of time. What we need to consider is our motivation for doing so. Are we doing kan-geiko this year because we're afraid our fellow dojo-mates won't accept us if we do not? Are we doing it because we are afraid of not doing it? Peer pressure and the demands of expectations within the group can be healthy forces. If they overwhelm our good sense and our sense of ourselves as individuals, they become destructive, and we need to rethink our motivations for participating in kan-geiko or in budo in general.

Societies have always had ways of testing oneself against the elements of nature, some formal, some more spontaneous. American Indian lore is full of episodes of young men taking off into the wilderness with minimal food or supplies. Today in Israel, men and women just out of their duty in the military there are expected to travel, both to see other parts of the world and to test themselves on their own. Indeed, it makes sense that much of the extreme nature of so many hobbies today—ice-climbing; base-jumping; surfing giant, potentially deadly waves—are a response to our modern world lacking formal rituals that serve to test us. In this context, kan-geiko is a way of doing just that. Through the regimen of a special period of training in the cold, the budoka has a clear goal. Can he make it up and into the dojo on a series of raw mornings, with its windows open to the bitter air, training barefoot on mats or a floor that is near freezing? Encouraged in part by the collective spirit and will of the group, and also by his own wish to see where his limits are, he gives it a try and finds, in most cases, he is capable of doing more than he thought. He learns that being cold and uncomfortable do not limit him. It's possible to take a barefoot run through snow without suffering nearly as much as he thought he might. From the outside, it may seem a little silly and macho. But the implications of kan-geiko are broad. If I can, without ill effect, train for two hours in temperatures I would normally consider too cold for taking the dog out for a walk, what else can I do that I thought would be beyond me? What are the real borders of my capabilities? Are they a little or a lot beyond what I have always believed them to be? These are the sorts of questions that get answered—or at least are asked—of the budoka during cold-weather practice.

Another element of kan-geiko has to do with the Shinto concept of self-purification, or *misogi*. Standing under icy waterfalls or wading waist-deep into frigid streams or waves at the ocean's side—these exercises have been a part of the rituals of Shinto priests or other anchorites in Japan for centuries. Modern budoka adopted them. More common in Japanese dojo than elsewhere, there are nevertheless training halls in this country where such strenuous ablutions are a part of the yearly cycle of the dojo. While their roots are religious, certainly not all participants in misogi rituals today embrace Shinto as a faith. Instead, they see these practices, usually accompanied by other training, as a way of facing oneself, looking inside to see what is there and to see how it might be best refined.

The opposite of kan-geiko is *natsu-geiko*, training at the height of summer. Natsu-geiko usually takes place in the latter part of July, during the hottest part of the season. Its aims and implications are exactly those of cold weather training. In between summer and winter training there will be other annual events in the dojo. Visiting instructors will come for special seminars. Periodically the dojo will be thoroughly cleaned. The early or late summer is often a time for *gasshuku*. The word means, to be billeted together as if staying in a dorm. Gasshuku in the budo refers to an intense period of training, from a weekend up to perhaps a week, in which members live together and train several hours a day. These sessions usually take place at resort areas or out in the country in Japan. In the United States, dojo will often rent a college dormitory and train either outside on the campus or in the gymnasium. Sometimes gasshuku are conducted so that trainees share in the duties of preparing meals; at others the food might be provided by the place where all are staying. The focus at gasshuku is not so much on teaching or learning new material as on practicing what's already been taught. There might be long runs through the countryside at a gasshuku each morning, or training on uneven ground, or other such activities that aren't a part of regular practice. Sometimes it will be members of several affiliated dojo devoted to the same art that get together. In any case, much of the value in gasshuku is spending a great deal of time with one's fellow practitioners. As important as the training at a gasshuku is the socializing that takes place during meals or in the evening. These are moments where members get to know one another better and learn how their seniors behave outside the training hall or, in the case of those seniors, gasshuku provide the opportunity to learn how to be a better leader and example.

All modern budo have some kind of ranking system and so of course testing is a regular part of the dojo year. Most forms of judo, karate-do, aikido, and kendo use the dan-i system, which in most cases is marked by the awarding of variously colored belts. The history of this method of ranking is discussed in the chapter on the keikogi; the details of it are noted in the chapter on the deshi. Testing for the next grade may come at regularly scheduled intervals or whenever the teacher feels it necessary. In some dojo, there may be *kyui betsu koshu,* or special classes devoted to the skills that a particular rank should have learned prior to testing for that rank. A *koshu* is a short course or "seminar." Sometimes koshu are directed at perfecting skills required for a certain rank. In addition to koshu aimed at specific ranks, there might be koshu in a number of other areas of the art as well. A teacher might schedule a koshu on etiquette in the dojo if he notices things have become sloppy in that area. In dojo where classical martial arts are taught, there might be koshu for demonstrating how armor was worn or repaired or on other such esoteric subjects that might not come up during normal practice. One popular koshu in dojo for modern budo is for applying the techniques of the art in the clothes practitioners would be wearing outside the dojo or for implementing them in difficult situations, like in a crowded room or in the dark.

Testing itself is called shinsa. It can be an informal affair, called without any warning, or it may be a special time for which the student prepares and appears before his teacher or a board of seniors to demonstrate his stuff. The announcement of the results of a shinsa is *happyo,* either read aloud to the assembled dojo or presented posted on the wall. If it is a good dojo, there will also be, following the testing, a *kaisetsu,* or explanation of the results. This is important if many students have failed at the examination, or if many have passed. Either way, they need to know why and by what criteria they were judged so they can plan for the next ranking.

Another part of the dojo year is *embu.* While *embu* means "a performance," in terms of the dojo, it typically refers to special demonstrations. During the year, the dojo may be asked to demonstrate their art publicly. There are appropriate places for a budo to be presented publicly: at cultural gatherings such as Japanese festivals, or for classes at a school learning about Japan or Japanese history or other events for disseminating Japanese culture, for example. And there are places—at movie premieres, mall openings, or other such places, where the budo will be presented more as a spectacle or entertainment than as a serious and dignified activity —that should never be considered appropriate for public demonstrations. A common way of referring to public demonstrations in Japanese is *shucho embu*. *Shucho* is an interesting word with an interesting historical derivation. Originally, it meant to deploy troops out on the battlefield in preparation for a fight. A related word is *shutsuba,* which means to ride one's horse out on to the battleground and take a stand. The budoka planning a public demonstration should think about this terminology. A presentation of one's art is certainly not the matter of life and death encountered on the field of battle. Still, it provides challenges that must be approached with sincerity and care.

Unless you are completely naïve, you must know that "martial arts" in the West have a connotation of unrestrained violence and machismo. Simultaneously, they are often thought of as a lot of ritualized silliness, bowing and yelping and striking ludicrous poses attired in weird costumes. An exhibition of budo must address these stereotypes. The exponents must try for a balance, showing the violence and conflict that are indeed at the heart of any fighting art; displaying, too, in the demonstration the "art," the aesthetic and beauty of movement that characterize these skills. In some instances, the dojo may wish to incorporate beginners in the demonstration to show that the art is not for super-humans. In others, they may decide to concentrate on the abilities of the more senior members, who can demonstrate the far range of expertise in the training hall. Those demonstrating, no matter what their level of skill, should be careful not to issue challenges or to insinuate that their art is without equal or one that will empower practitioners with fantastic talents. There will eventually be someone in the crowd who will take exception to such absurd claims and then you will be on the spot.

Another danger in demonstrating a budo is that someone can easily be hurt. Injury is always a threat in the dojo. No matter how careful, people can be hurt. The chances of this can increase in a public embu. Those demonstrating are apt to be nervous, pumped full of adrenaline by the excitement of the presentation, and likely to be going faster and harder than they might in normal practice. These tendencies have to be addressed firmly by the teacher or leader of the demonstration before it happens. You are demonstrating your art because you are proud of it or because in one way or another you believe it worth showing. A dazzling demonstration, perfectly executed, will be completely overshadowed by the fact that someone had to be helped off the embu-jo, or demonstration area, with a broken limb or a bloody face.

In contrast to a public shucho embu is the *hono embu,*

which takes place almost inevitably in private, either within the confines of the dojo or, in Japan, at some site that has deep spiritual significance to the art. A *hono* is an offering in a religious sense, or a "dedication." Hono embu are demonstrations not intended for others but for the spirits of one's ancestors in the budo. A hono embu occurs at certain times of the year that have some meaning for the art or the school. They are conducted, as with normal training in the dojo, before the kamidana. In Japan, they make take place at Shinto shrines or other areas such as cemeteries or locations where the spirits of the ancestors in the art are brought to mind. A hono embu is a formal event. Kimono might be worn in some cases. If not, there will still be a sense of solemnity about the affair. In some dojo, only senior members will participate in a hono embu, or maybe even only the teacher and his most senior student. In others, the entire membership will be expected to participate. All demonstrate as though their ancestors are present. They perform to their very best, as if to show how much they appreciate what has been handed down through the generations. A hono embu can be held only once a year or even less often. But if hono embu are not performed in a dojo, one must wonder about the seriousness of the place or the historical connections its members have with the founder and earlier generations of their art. Sometimes this embu will not have an outward appearance of being what it is. At the Kodokan's annual Kagami Biraki celebration in January each year, there is a formal demonstration of judo's kata that many see as simply that: a presentation of techniques by top-level judoka. In reality, this is a hono embu. The judo demonstrations there may be impressive for spectators to watch. Their purpose, though, is not to impress or entertain the crowd but for exponents to present their art to the spirits of those who have gone before them in the world of judo.

Keiko osame is the last training session of the year. It happens in December, of course, often right in the middle of preparations for the New Year festivities in the dojo, around the twenty-eighth of the month. It is not a formal aspect of the dojo year in most places. In some dojo it will not even be remarked upon at all. Japanese culture and the observance of various moments in the course of the season are full of examples of the celebration of the first things. The first full moon of autumn, for instance, or the first fresh bonito caught: these are ritually noted. The last of things, however, are rarely given much attention. In some dojo already cleaned and polished for the coming new year there might be a final sweeping, called *susuharai*. Susuharai is carried out in homes and businesses in Japan, a ceremonial sweeping of the floor that is supposed to clear the place of any motes of misfortune that might be collecting—like small, unnoticed dust bunnies—in the corners and crannies. Aside from that, most students and teachers are too busy with the coming festivities of the New Year to think much about keiko osame. Perhaps there will be a budoka, more thoughtful than others, who will pause at the end of the last bow of the year, to reflect for a moment. Another year gone. Another year's worth of memories, good times, and times of frustration and hardship. Injuries may have been encountered, requiring time to heal. Limitations may have been exceeded; you may have gone places further than you believed possible when the year started. Or, you may feel the gnawing worry and anxiety that you are no further along than you were twelve months ago, that you are stuck and are repeating the same mistakes again and again. (In terms of following a martial Way, the sense one is decidedly *not* going anywhere is a far more important part of the going at some stages than the going itself.) What were you working on a year ago at this time? Does it still confound you? Or have you moved so far ahead of where you were then that you cannot even remember what were, a year ago, terrific obstacles? And whether you have significantly moved forward in your training or not, what will next year bring?

Keiko osame means "the end of training," or "the last training." Of course, the end of the year in the dojo, the final class of the year, means nothing of the sort. There is no "end." And in another sense, there is no "next." There is only the moment. There is the effort and commitment one has put into *this* practice, this session. The calendar has been turned another page; the seasons have circled around once again. What has remained steady, though, is that student, linked to the past and pulled simultaneously into the future but who, for the moment, is right where he is—and who knows that that is right where he needs and wishes to be.

GLOSSARY

aite   An opponent or practice partner during train-
              ing. An aite is not an "enemy," but rather some-
              one acting in an antagonistic role as part of the
              training process.

bokken   A wooden sword used as a substitute for the steel
              version of the weapon used in training, and that
              was also used as a weapon itself during the feudal
              period.

bokuto   See *bokken*.

budo   The Way of Japan's martial arts. The word can
              imply not only a means of physical training but
              a spiritual or aesthetic pursuit as well.

buki   The generic Japanese term for weapons.

chado   The Way of the tea ceremony.

dan   A grade or level formally recognized within an
              art. In some budo forms, this may be done
              through the awarding of a colored belt, and
              where it is, the black belt typically signifies the
              first grade of the dan ranks.

dan-i   The ranking or grading system of an art that usually uses belts as an indication of one's rank. See also *menkyo*.

deshi   A student.

do   Literally, a "path" or "road," *Do* refers to an art, with the implication of spiritual or aesthetic dimensions that underlie the purely physical aspects of its curriculum.

dogu   The equipment, or *gu,* used in following a *do,* or Way.

dohai   A person training with you in the same dojo or art who is more or less equal in status, having commenced his training at the same time you did. See also *kohai* and *sempai*.

hanshi   A title conferred on a senior practitioner of an art, often one that carries with it the status of a teacher.

heigo   Literally, "martial language." Heigo is the idiom of martial or military training and life, including a number of terms often used in the dojo.

ikebana   The Way of flower arranging.

in-yo   The Japanese pronunciation of the Chinese characters for "yin" and "yang."

isshin-denshin The direct transmission of skills or information between a teacher and a student.

kami   Ancestral, communal, or indigenous "spirits" or deities within the context of Shinto religion or folk practice.

kata	Exercise forms designed to integrate specific neuromuscular motor skills in the practitioner of an art.
keikogi	A generic term for the clothes worn while practicing some form of budo.
kohai	A junior within an art or dojo. See also *sempai*.
koryu	Literally, "old traditions." *Koryu* is a very broad term used to describe martial arts systems originating before the end of Japan's feudal era in 1867.
kyoshi	One of several titles conferred upon practitioners with advanced skills or experience within an art, often implying some kind of teaching authority.
menkyo	A "license" given within an art. Most modern forms of budo do not use menkyo gradings, but they are common in older forms.
monjin	Literally, a "person at the gate." *Monjin* is a word used to describe a beginner or hopeful entrant to an art.
mudansha	Literally, "person without rank." *Mudansha* usually describes practitioners of an art who have not yet attained any rank or who have not yet been awarded a dan rank. See also *yudansha*.
nage	A term applied in those arts that include grappling with or throwing an opponent, which refers to the person doing the action. See also *uke*.

reishiki	Etiquette.
renshi	A title for a more advanced practitioner, one that often indicates the receiver has been granted permission to teach some or all aspects of an art.
ryu	Written with the character that means "flowing," *ryu* is the term for a distinct system or tradition of an art.
semete	A term used in arts that involve percussive techniques, *semete* indicates the person performing the action. See also *ukete*.
sempai	A senior within the dojo or art. See also *kohai*.
shidachi	A term used, particularly in martial arts or Ways that feature the use of weapons, to indicate the person who is receiving or reacting to a threat or attack. He is, ideally, the person meant to successfully deal with the encounter. See also *uchidachi*.
shidoin	A title awarded that indicates some level of teaching responsibility in an art or dojo.
soke	The founder of an art.
uchidachi	The person initiating an attack in a practice session. See also *shidachi*.
uke	The person "receiving" an attack or offensive action while training. See also *nage*.

ukete   Literally, the "receiving hand." *Ukete* refers to the person at whom an attack is directed and who is expected, in the training process, to deal with it. See also *semete*.

yudansha   A person who has received a dan grade. See also *mudansha*.